Call of the Ancient Mariner

Call of the Ancient Mariner

Reese Palley's Guide to a Long Sailing Life

Reese Palley

 International Marine / McGraw-Hill

Camden, Maine • New York • Chicago • San Francisco
Lisbon • London • Madrid • Mexico City • Milan • New Delhi
San Juan • Seoul • Singapore • Sydney • Toronto

The *McGraw·Hill* Companies

1 2 3 4 5 6 7 8 9 10 DOC DOC 0 9 8 7 6 5 4 3

The following sections were previously published in altered form: "The Most Dangerous Orifice," in *Cruising World* (May 1998), "A New Breed," in *Sail Magazine* (April 1999), "No One to Speak for the Stars," in *Good Old Boat* (July/August 2000), "Old Sailors Get It Right," in *Cruising World* (August 1997), "One Against the Gods," in *Cruising World* (September 1995), "The Secret Joys of Sailing," in *Cruising World* (1998), "Why Not Just Cut Out My Heart," in *Cruising World* (June 2003).

Excerpt on page vi of "Intuition" by R. Buckminster Fuller © The Estate of R. Buckminster Fuller; reprinted with permission.

Library of Congress Cataloging-in-Publication Data
Palley, Reese.
  Call of the ancient mariner : Reese Palley's guide to a long sailing life / Reese Palley.
     p.   cm.
  ISBN 0-07-138881-8
  1. Boats and boating—Miscellanea. 2. Aged—Recreation—Miscellanea. 3. Palley, Reese. I. Title.
  GV777.3.P35 2003
  797.1—dc21   2003013532

Questions regarding the content of this book should be addressed to
International Marine
P.O. Box 220
Camden, ME 04843
www.internationalmarine.com

Questions regarding the ordering of this book should be addressed to
The McGraw-Hill Companies
Customer Service Department
P.O. Box 547
Blacklick, OH 43004
Retail customers: 1-800-262-4729
Bookstores: 1-800-722-4726

Photographs of the author and Fred Schwall by Marilyn Arnold Palley; photograph of Humphrey and Mary Barton by Mary Barton; other Ancient Mariner photographs courtesy of the person photographed.

Young love
To this old sailor
Came with truth and passion.
Boundless joy given
Boundless joy received.
In small compense
I dedicate this work
To
Marilyn.

Intuition

And of all the designs
Thus far formulated by humans
None have been
As adequately anticipatory
Of probable reoccurrences
Of yesterdays experiences—
Positive and negative,
Large and small,
Frequent and infrequent,
Sudden and slow,
And therefore as
Progressively comprehensive,
Complexedly adequate,
Economically exquisite,
Powerfully eloquent
And regeneratively reinspiring
To further evolutionary perfection
As is
The sailing ship

—R. Buckminster Fuller

from Ulysses

The lights begin to twinkle from the rocks;
The long day wanes; the slow moon climbs; the deep
Moans round with many voices. Come, my friends.
'T is not too late to seek a newer world.
Push off, and sitting well in order smite
The sounding furrows; for my purpose holds
To sail beyond the sunset, and the baths
Of all the western stars, until I die.
It may be that the gulfs will wash us down;
It may be we shall touch the Happy Isles,
And see the great Achilles, whom we knew.
Tho' much is taken, much abides; and tho'
We are not now that strength which in old days
Moved earth and heaven, that which we are, we are,—
One equal temper of heroic hearts,
Made weak by time and fate, but strong in will
To strive, to seek, to find, and not to yield.

—Alfred Tennyson

CONTENTS

INTRODUCTION

Why Don't You Just Tear Out My Heart?

Old and achey though I be
I still thirst for wind and sea
And foreign shores to leave behind
As I unwind
The tangle of my life.
—Reese Palley

Marilyn, my wife and shipmate, came to me as I was relaxing in the Key West sun without a care in the world and said, "Reese, you are not going to like this, but . . ."

I quickly cut her off as storm clouds blotted the sun and great seas rose threateningly in my mind. What could she have to say, I wondered . . . divorce? Hardly, since we had already survived a trip down that road. A bad medical report on me? No, I had just come clean with my doctors. So it had to be that we'd been wiped out by the market.

It wasn't that. It was worse . . . much worse. "Reese," she said, "you have just turned eighty [as if I had to be reminded], and I really think [here it comes] that our boat is too big for us."

The bottom dropped out of my world as I heard the words I never wanted to hear but that I knew were all too true. Marilyn was suggesting that the time had come to cast out my heart, my soul—our 46-foot Ted Brewer one-off, *Unlikely*, which had sailed us safely around the world in an eighteen-year circumnavigation, perhaps the longest on record.

There's a sailor's saying that the two happiest days are the day you get your new boat and the day you sell your old one. Nothing could be less true in my case. My very persona, my self-esteem, was tied up in sailing in general and in *Unlikely* in particular.

One of the troubles that comes with growing old is that you simply can't do at eighty what you did at forty (no snickering, please). A 46-foot, 20-ton round-the-world cruiser requires lots of muscle. Everything aboard gets heavier with each foot of waterline you add. You need chain . . . lots of heavy, recalcitrant chain and hundreds of feet of equally heavy nylon rode. The anchors on *Unlikely*, designed to hold in a hurricane (as they had on more than one occasion), went down to the bottom real fast but came up with enormous reluctance. The sails, and *Unlikely* has many strong sails, would take the starch out of an Atlas.

But the weight of gear wasn't the only reason that Marilyn spoke the unspeakable. *Unlikely* has a 6-foot draft, and the entrance from the sea to our dock in the Keys is only 5 feet, 11 inches. Only on full-moon high tide could we enter or leave, and even then we scraped paint off the keel. That meant we could sail out, with difficulty, once a month and would have to wait another month to sail back in. This circumstance somewhat limited our use of our beloved boat.

In spite of all of these impediments to sailing, and in spite of the crystalline logic that our boat had to go, I wasn't sure that my ego, my sense of myself, would survive looking out the window at our seawall and not seeing *Unlikely* there.

But sweet Marilyn, knowing that she was about to destroy me, threw me a lifeline. "What," she asked, "do you love so much about *Unlikely*?"

"Well," I replied, "first, I've become used to Ted Brewer's design. I know what he builds into a boat, and his ideas have never let me down. I know that our boat is a survival craft and that short of some major stupidity on my part she will carry, and has carried, us through events that would have blanched my hair had it not already been whitened by age. Second, I like a heavy boat that can carry us and plenty of supplies across any ocean we seek to challenge. Third, I love the 13-foot beam of *Unlikely* and the comfort that it gives. Fourth, I still want to have the highest mast in port."

"How about three out of four?" she urged. I knew I'd been trapped, but still I had to ask. "What do I lose?" "Five feet off the top of the mast," she replied. "And the rest?" I asked.

"A 38-foot Ted Brewer design, weighing less than half of *Unlikely*, built with the solid and dependable long keel you claim grips the ocean like a leech and with 12 feet of beam; in short, just as capable for a blue-water passage as is *Unlikely*."

"What impossible boat is that?" I asked, knowing I was being led farther down the garden path.

"A Morgan 38." I was done for.

Once I was faced with the inevitable, Marilyn's proposal started to look possible. I could still claim to be an ocean passagemaker (even if the passages were now few and far between) as I would have a blue-water capable boat.

Unlikely, which we had kept in Bristol fashion for twenty years, ready in a New York minute for any far horizon that beckoned, would simply have to become someone else's magic carpet.

Over the years since we built her we've put three times her original purchase price back into her and Lord only knows how many years of sweat and toil, so you can be damn sure that I won't allow any Tom, Dick, or Cocktail Suzy to have her.

No, Sir!

There will be interviews, quizzes, and absolute guarantees that she will still cross oceans. That's what *Unlikely* was born to do, and while taking her away from me will tear out my heart, I can't abide destroying her leaping spirit by denying her the distant shores of sailing.

No, Sir. I may have to let her go, but I still must know she's somewhere at sea, safely and solidly carrying some other sentimental fool in pursuit of his dreams.

As I began to accept the inevitable, it dawned on me that I wasn't all that unique in my discomfort, that there must be thousands of other sailors graduating, or about to graduate, from cockpit to sofa, away from the sea. And there must be many thousands more, still young and very much involved with the world, who yearn for a retirement to the sea. Here was a constituency that could profit from a guide to how to be an old sailor. As I thought about it, there seemed to be much more than just guidance needed. Sailor folk, young and old, those still at sea and those recently departed from it, need not merely a guidebook but a manifesto. We need not only a "how to do it"—we need a strong argument for "why to do it at all."

We must put aside the temerity of the young and accept the risk that it is a bit more dangerous to be an Ancient Mariner than a young and nimble one. We ancients move slower, hurt more, and eke out our stamina with a niggardly hand. We are clearly handicapped by age no less than a sailor with one leg or no legs, and there have been many of these. All of us, one way or another, are handicapped either physically or emotionally or, indeed, intellectually. Once we glance about us and take a measure of our poor, sad, and mostly inadequate peers, our own handicap of too many decades turns into something akin to pride that we made it at all and are still making it!

So, sans eyes, sans teeth, sans strength of limb, as long as we can tumble over the safety lines and clutch onto the deck, we have an obligation to our great age to keep putting our ancient asses into the wet and cold and endless tumult of the sea. Since we've lived too many years already, is it really so damned important not to risk one or two of these years for one more exalting, mind-bending, ineluctable moment of careless intoxication that is the gift the sea so freely offers? A princely, munificent gift offered only to our band of lucky sailors? A gift that it would be shameful and knavish to refuse?

Thus this manifesto for Ancient Mariners was born.

People die these days as much from boredom and irrelevance as from disease. Antiquarian depression is pandemic in America. To help others avoid so depressing a fate, this handbook shares with the reader the experiences of this Ancient Mariner. There are obvious adjustments to be made as physical and mental facilities alter and falter. Herein are tips and tricks to keep you sailing decades after you might have thought you were through with the sea. For a sailor, being through with the sea is like being through with life itself. "Choose life" and continue to choose the sea.

Much of what is discussed here is simple common sense that, in truth, applies to the young sailor as well as the old. All are equal at some level, but in Orwellian terms, "Old sailors are more equal than others." Your good genes, with the help of incessant physical activity, abstinence from tobacco and fat, and assisted by a cornucopia of medical miracles, can sail you into what used to be called old age.

The best advice is that which, in repetition, does not appear silly. I gladly risk reader boredom by reiterating stuff I consider central and important. None of us learn easily, and rote may still be an effective way to hammer crucial information into our thick and, in the case of "old farts," thickening skulls.

Mar and I have made a hubric pact to write our next book in 2012 when I turn ninety. Given a huge dollop of luck and a blessing from whoever masters the universe . . . we'll see you then.

Keep sailing.

We Ain't Dead Yet

Consign Me to the Seas

When I no longer share
Summer's air with you,
Consign me to the seas,
Where I may love you on any shore.

I have spent a lifetime inveighing against the dangers of solo sailing. And then appears a remarkable antique, Captain David Clark, who validates this book with his epic solo world circumnavigation. An octogenarian, David is the oldest solo circumnavigator on record.

The last time I spoke to David he was planning a jaunt to the Bahamas and Bermuda with the clear intent of going around the planet again. —Reese

Dave Clark on Voyaging

I returned from my last solo circumnavigation eight months ago, making me, in all probability, the oldest of all solo circumnavigators.

I'm in excellent shape, especially considering I have lived through eight decades. I attribute my age and viability to my life on the high seas. At sea, whether I want to be or not, I'm in  a constant state of exercise, even if it's nothing more than just hanging on. I'm convinced that is part of the reason for my remaining fit.

But it's much more than that! Not only is it important for all of us at *any* age to exercise physically, but, more importantly, we all need to have a proper perspective and correct mental attitude in our lives. I think we all need to find our personal directions and live our lives consistently with our natures.

I know it is life on the high seas that fits my nature most precisely. I can't answer why this is so; I only know that I'm most content and most "with it" when I'm making long passages or just living on my boat.

I miss my wife and my family very much when I'm on these long voyages, and I absolutely abhor bad weather, and frankly I'm not crazy about boats, but I love what they enable me to do. I've seen many countries. I've met delightful people in all walks of life. I'm a member of a unique fraternity of long-range cruising people who are supportive of one another. I've met and overcome some difficult challenges that have made me stronger and more self-sufficient. I've seen some of the most gorgeous and incredible sunsets and sunrises, so beautiful they defy description. I've had the experience of watching the vague and dim outline of a new country or exotic shore begin to emerge and take shape after a passage of thirty or forty days and have discovered that most people in most countries are gracious, friendly, and courteous if we behave in a like manner.

All of the above is true, and yet it barely touches the experiences I've been able to enjoy as a long-range cruising sailor. Even more important, at least to me, is the freedom sailors can find at sea, which is simply not to be had amid the restraints and clamors of land.

We sailors are, literally and figuratively, the captains of our lives. We chart and plot our courses through life, and we're free to go when, where, and if we so choose, unshackled by the societal constraints of the land dweller.

This isn't a recommendation for anyone else, but it fits my nature. As in any other way of life, there are plenty of negatives, but from my perspective the positives far outweigh them!

Of course, there are dangers and some risks, but what kind of a life would it be if there weren't a bit of daring in each of us? I'm not so afraid of dying as I am of not living while I'm here.

—*David B. Clark, Captain of the* Mickey, *2002*

We Ain't Dead Yet

I picked up the phone the other day and called Captain David Clark. David is one of those few people who truly earn the sobriquet *Captain* as, even in his eighties, he still solo circumnavigates the world. If you're reading this book in sequence, you will have just met Dave.

When I asked him how he was doing, David replied, "We ain't dead yet!"

"We Ain't Dead Yet" sounds like a good title for this book, as does "Old Farts in the Wind," another title rejected by my thoughtful publishers. They claim, and I believe them, that they know the book market better than I do.

Both titles have a stringent honesty and directness about them. Both are iconoclastic, and both leapt from the mouths of old sailors. Most important, both are pregnant with the salty wisdom of folk who have been long at sea.

I started this book with the intent of teaching old sailors a thing or two about the sailorly life. I have ended up learning more than I taught. All I needed to do was to keep my mouth shut and nurse a silent beer as I listened.

Old sailors, I have discovered, are enthusiastic recounters of sea adventures, each of which has a lesson for the listener. Their salty tales remind all sailors that there just is no excuse based on age for not going to sea.

I have also discovered that among the hundreds of sailors I've interviewed there was absolute unanimity about the glories and benefits of the sailorly life, but no two could agree on why they chose sailing.

All said that they were "driven" to the sea, but the "why" escaped explication. In the end they, and I, all had to revert to an expression of pure faith. We all know how gloriously the sailorly life impacts us, but the "why" remains unanswered and unanswerable.

All unanimously agreed on one true thing: that sailing after sixty is the way to stay physically, mentally, and emotionally alive. I couldn't find even one old sailor still at sea who regretted being there. Among those who remained at sea with debilitating physical handicaps, the general opinion is that what would kill them at sea would just as likely kill them on land—actually more likely, since they wouldn't enjoy the stringent physical toning a sailing vessel produces.

While old sailors easily tell the stories of their adventures, few can deal with their feelings as solo sailor Bernard Moitessier did. It's the murky fogs of feeling and emotion that are the great gift of the sea. We may not be able to make young sailors understand the wild shores of emotional experiences through which we've passaged, but all of us, myself included, nurse the deep and satisfying knowledge that we have plumbed emotional deeps not available to the landbound. We Ancient Mariners are a breed apart from those anchored to the land.

No, we ain't dead yet.

In Praise of Irresponsibility

The looming problem of being young is that, lest you be labeled a bum, hobo, or hippie, you're obligated to do the world's work. These are all labels of opprobrium of various tints, which we of the West, puritans all, despise. We choose to give our lives to the clock rather than to follow our Maker's natural laws. By the time we escape from school, we've acquired, willy-nilly, a smothering cape of responsibility and the inexplicable need to turn from the natural inclination to laze about to an unnatural enslavement to a 9-to-5 existence.

Then, as we near age sixty, a small miracle occurs that, alas, too few of us have the wit to recognize. We're relieved from the importuning of progeny now fully grown, our competitiveness abates, and it dawns on us that we have inadvertently acquired two surprising gifts. First, unless we've been extraordinarily unlucky, most of us have acquired a small but adequate retirement income. Second, we've now inherited the true fruit of all of our labored, responsible, and constricting years—namely, the time to do as we damn well please. The days of our lives are now replete with hours that aren't found on the face of a clock, in the squeals of infants, or in the urgent demands of an overbearing superior. We now have money and time . . . both, for the first time in our lives, at the same time.

Free at last!

Free at last?

Hardly. Some few of us have the sapient long-headedness to recognize this precious gift of freedom and turn away from the world, from progeny, and from dulling friends toward the proper usage of time . . . discovery of a new life.

Most do not, however, and the cry of boredom rises above the herd. Cats and dogs, when bored, sleep. People complain, and instead of turning delicious, unscheduled moments to account, we constrict horizons, deflate physiques, and unstretch our minds and bodies with bridge or golf or television.

Retirement mustn't mean the end of work. Retirement should mean escaping from a dulling regimen of unwanted work and reborning into new life and new work. I retired from the world thirty years ago and have never worked harder in my life. What I did with my life became *my* choice, not *theirs*. In this newfound freedom I discovered rich and creative reserves that had been hidden beneath blankets of responsibility.

Matt had a heart attack and was forced into unwanted retirement at seventy. He had once been an engineer and then had graduated into the structuring of real-estate developments. He was rigidly responsible and disciplined, a condition that might be expected from an engineer. In retirement he went from the demands of punctuality and deadlines to a soft and amorphous state of endless, unfilled time . . . and little to fill it. Within a year, those who loved him began to see emotional deterioration. Matt missed the discipline that his work had required, and more even than that, Matt missed the sense of responsibilities met that comes with doing the world's work.

He was well on his way to his second, and we feared fatal, heart attack.

One morning, realizing that the sailorly life would be too late aborning for Matt, I appeared bearing a gift . . . a computer. Matt, who had never touched a computer, proved a quick study. Once he got the hang of it, he started to write small, personal observations about his immediate experiences. He proved to have a lovely talent for irony and a quick eye for the small character flaws that beset most of us. Matt had found a new life, new purpose in his writing. Most importantly, Matt discovered he no longer needed to be responsibly constrained *inside* the tent . . . he now could wander freely about outside and be as critical and irresponsible as he chose.

Matt's pieces were a great success. They were bought (usually for modest sums) and published. The writing changed Matt's sense of self. During his last years this dedicated engineer, when asked what he did, would answer with seemly pride, "I am a writer."

There is a bittersweet, O'Henry twist to this tale. Matt's pieces usually earned him around $50, usual for the genre. Two weeks after he died his widow received a check for $500, an enormous sum under the circumstances, for an article he had submitted months before. Matt missed this sanctioning, this substantiation of his newfound sense of self. Perhaps we can hope that deep down he did know . . . every time he answered, "I am a writer."

The decades of elderhood, like Matt's, must be untrammeled seas of excitement in which all schedules are blank. What we do and when we do it in these years, when we leave and when we come, with whom we consort and, more importantly, with whom we do not, are matters, *if you are a sailor*, strictly between you and the random delights of nature.

Of all the many ways to retire healthily, life asea seems best to fit the sailorly order of things. The absence of too much money and the presence of too much time match the measured and stately progress of a sailing vessel, which rarely goes faster than you can walk and mostly, if you are careful, costs you half what you would spend to retire onshore.

A sailorly life demands the banishing of artificial timetables. Schedules are now only the measured rise and fall of tides, the vagaries of currents, and the serendipity of Aeolus. Young folk, with noses to the grindstone, lack the slippery ease of the old when it comes to evading schedules and responsibilities. The lives of the young are set in the concrete demands of an unfeeling, and in most part inhuman, social contract. We elders, if we are wise, abrogate that contract, smash the clock, and, in the best possible sense, inherit the wind.

In all my sailing years, in all my passages, whether they were across a bay or across a vast sea, I have only rarely arrived at the destination planned and have never arrived there in the anticipated time. I've learned to live by *toward* and *whenever*, conditions that only we irresponsible ancients can achieve with comfort and dignity.

The true gift of aging is time, and the true gift of time is the epiphanic flash that the irresponsibility of free hours, days, and years is our ultimate reward for surviving the self-imposed stringencies of society.

A Debt to Coasting

Days of nepenthe on the blue seas do not come easily. The spiritual gifts of the great oceans are made possible by the hard work and learning that can be accomplished only in the shallow and challenging waters just outside your own home port.

In excursions alongshore, close to home, we pass enchanting and rewarding days honing our sailorly skills. Roaring powerboats, shallows that reach for your keel, eddies and currents that move you in unwanted directions, winds that are twisted and magnified by the land off which they blow, lee shores, and big, scary freighters traversing narrow waterways all conspire to etch the skills of sailing indelibly into your psyche.

Alongshore is where you delight in the knowledge of *exactly* where you are at every moment, compared to blue-water sailing where *approximately* is plenty good enough. An error of a foot or two can complicate life in shallow waters, while an *oops!* of a handful of miles in the deeps results in little more than a moment of embarrassment.

After two decades of wandering the globe, *Unlikely* needed to be refit. Since we had aged more quickly than she, we needed a vessel that was smaller, more nimble, and with less draft. We could hardly refit our own bodies to new circumstances as well as we could refit our vessel. *Unlikely* would have to give way to the exigencies of age, and since we weren't planning to cross too many more serious oceans, we prepared *Unlikely*, like a bride, for her new master.

For the twelve months it took us to rebuild and restore her for sale, we were without a sailboat. As we labored on *Unlikely*, we watched a nifty 38-foot sloop slip by us every day for some daysailing off the Keys. At the helm was a weathered old sea dog, and on the foredeck was his lively, octogenarian wife, both hale and happy. They passed us with a wave, beaming with that special, anticipatory smile that wreaths the faces of sailors as they reach eagerly for a day at sea. Each evening they returned, anticipation fulfilled. It became a special sort of torture for us, as we yearned to be off for our own day at sea, freed from the tasks and confrontations and shackles of land.

As I jealously watched the salty grandame and grandsire take to the sea each day, I realized that the deep seas for me were a thing of the past, as are the deep seas for most old sailors. Times change, bodies and capabilities change, and now, in my ninth decade, I still wanted my life at sea. From my new perspective of great age, a week along a pleasant shore, or even a day, looked just as delicious as a forty-day passage to the French Marquesas once had.

On an ocean passage the first navlight you are likely to see may be a month away, and navigational marks, defining depths and dangers, are encountered only after you raise your first lighthouse. Sailing a great ocean misses much of the high excitement of keeping your vessel safe from the hazards of shallows and lee shores. Deep at sea you have the leisure to quest after sensate activities that turn the mind inward. Close alongshore, the physical senses are galvanized, and sailing skills are honed for the pleasing reward of bringing your vessel safely and elegantly home.

While coastal sailing is demanding and difficult, there is, in even the shortest sail in familiar waters, the continuing exaltation of problems solved. Coasting is like a crossword puzzle in which every action, every decision, becomes part of the mosaic of the entire experience during which you meld yourself to your vessel. Daysailing is a participatory sport, while ocean sailing, for the largest portion of your time at sea, is a spectator sport.

Coastal sailing is the quicksilver, instant, heart-pounding delight of contest. It grants those pellucid moments of gestalt when puzzles and challenges flash clear, and you sense growth in yourself as a sailor. Ocean sailing is contemplative, slow, and introspective, requiring minimal skill and strength but deeply challenging the spirit and emotions. Passing across a great ocean is a precious reward, the *goal* of the sailorly life for many. Coastal sailing is *process*, and some would argue that process itself is reward aplenty.

One of these two modalities of sailing looks to Eastern thought, and the other to Western. Ocean passagemaking is essentially Zen, timeless, passive, placid, and thoughtful. Alongshore sailing is essentially Western, dynamic, momentary, active, outward seeking. They are obverse and reverse of the same coin. If you miss one experience, you diminish the other. The irony for sailors young and old who seek far horizons is that there is no choice at all, since without the exigent lessons of coastal sailing we would either never get out to sea or, if we did, we might well not survive.

Young sailors must hone their inshore skills so they're prepared for the landfalls in their future. Old sailors, both those who've sailed the blue oceans and those who've found their dreams closer to home, can, in the lengthened lives now granted, ease their sheets and have instant and delicious escape from the noxious congregants and regimentations of our crowded land.

To call yourself *sailor*, all you need do is cast off your docklines. Whether you're seeking the far shores or a marina just around the point, you need the same sailorly skills for both, and for both the dreamy mindset of the adventurer.

Pacing

Almost all avocations and recreations begin by demanding a high expenditure of energy. Running sports, jumping sports, and pure feats-of-strength sports all impose extraordinary demands on physical and aerobic stamina.

Excellence in these activities peaks in youth and diminishes, almost to extinction, as one reaches sixty. The only sporting activity that maintains a level drain on energy from beginning to end is sailing.

The first time you take tiller in hand you are made aware that sailing requires no extraordinary dexterity and very little aerobic capacity, and only in moments of high crisis, which occur blessedly seldomly, does sailing require any great strength. So you can literally sail forever and be as good at it at ninety as you were half a century earlier.

Despite this, or perhaps because the expenditure of energy is smooth, regular, and nonabusive, sailing is demonstrably the healthiest of sports.

Granted, there are some activities on a boat with which the old sailor must take care. But they have little to do with actual sailing and much to do with the endless and demanding labor that any vessel requires to keep it seaworthy.

If you choose to maintain your vessel yourself, the key word is *pacing*. I recently had to tear down some hundreds of strips of wood lining the ceilings of my boat. My choice was to pay $45 an hour for what was essentially grunt work, or to do it myself.

The first day on the job was a disaster. I spent six exhausting hours in a very hot boat with my arms over my head tearing out reluctant and resistant structures. I'd forgotten my age and, as a result, paid the piper over the next week. When I finally was able to get back to the job, I reminded myself of my eight decades and spent two civilized hours a day for the next four days on the work. The deed was done without killing myself.

I had paced the job, which, because it was taken slowly and in small nonabusive bites, was better done.

Pacing is also applicable to passage lengths. When you're sixty or seventy, a transatlantic passage is a perfectly reasonable proposition. At seventy to eighty it's time to putter about in the Caribbean, wander about in the Bahamas, or pop over to Cuba for a bit of the high life.

At eighty to ninety your choice of passage is problematical and very personal. Some of us, luckier in our choice of parents than most, will still contemplate far horizons, while others will prefer the many charms of daysailing.

The matter remains all about pacing. Be realistic about your own capabilities, yet beware of underestimating that marvelous physical mechanism that has carried you well into old age. You're capable of more than you think. And if you don't try, if you avoid all paths that wind in harm's way . . . well, you'll never know, will you?

Be especially resistant to what other folk *think* you should be doing. What they *might* well feel is that you should be in an old-age anteroom for the cemetery. Never, never allow vox populi to make life decisions for you.

The Feel of Childhood

"A sailor's joys are as simple as a child's."

Thus spoke Bernard Moitessier in *The Long Way*, a book by an old sailor that conveys more of the *joys* of sailing than the usually dull *business* of sailing.

His ebullient recantations of small thrills and large personal revelations are familiar to anyone who has sailed the deep oceans. His pleasure in a bird, a fish, a wisp of air after a calm, is really what ocean sailing is about. How dull is the business of "where I went" and "how I did it." What an old ocean sailor cares about is how he *feels* at sea, not what he thinks. Even less should we care what he knows. He may know how old he is, but as with Moitessier, his feelings recall his youth.

The transfer of sailorly information takes place between the sailor and his living vessel, not between a sailor and any book that has ever been written. It's his ship that teaches the lubber to become a sailor. After ten days and a thousand miles at sea, a learning process sets in that simply can't be conveyed in print. What you read about sail handling is parsecs distant from the learning that takes place as old muscles sense the tension and liveliness of the pull of the sheets.

Even less can be read about that instinctive tugging and tucking that takes place as you reef in a rising breeze. True, an old sailor can pass along tricks and techniques, but that stuff only goes into your head . . . what is necessary is sailing lore that goes directly into your muscles.

One of the truly great joys of sailing, as Moitessier knew in his bones, is the melding and merging that joins skipper to tiller to vessel. Each dip and wallow, each pull and release, impart volumes of information to muscles and heart . . . so much information that, were it routed through his brain, it would only stunt the sailor's fathom of the manner in which he must deal with the sea. Synapses between heart and gut are an order of magnitude greater than those inside our slow and bumbling brains. The stuff you learn in your muscles is never unremembered . . . learning sailorly skills is like learning to ride a bicycle; you can't be taught it by others, you're almost unaware of learning to ride, and you're incapable of forgetting.

The old ocean sailor recaptures those joys of childhood when every taste was new and every vision unique, and when learning of the world came as a blinding rush that melted into revelation. The simple joys of childhood emerge from the newness of each experience. It's the lovely gift of sailing that reinvents newness for the sailor. It's precisely this reincarnation that is the great gift of the sea to Ancient Mariners.

Experiences on land that have become dulled with familiarity, old and boring ways of sensing the miracles around and within us, are renewed in the aptly named "cradle" of the sea. We sailors, especially we senescent sailors, are offered the inestimable gift of rebirth. We are Botticelli's Venus emerging from the sea, newly made, fresh, and, even if only in our minds, beautiful and filled with the beauty about us.

Like children, we old sailors lose our sense of time. A week, a month, is the same as a moment in a day when something extraordinary happens at sea. Like children, we sailors on long ocean passages have no intimidating sense of future, only the endless rolling of the seas beneath us that promises to go on forever. As with children, time for us has no stop. Our senses are disoriented by the separation from land, cares, and depressing eventualities. Old sailors are granted a limited immortality while at sea, a doubling of the life experiences of nonsailorly folk.

The names we give our boats speak of hope and future. We name our boats as children name the unseen, imagined playmates of their secret and unseen lives. My own vessel, *Unlikely*, was named when I sensed how strange it was that I, overweight, overage, overmortgaged, and overburdened with cares of family, was about to set out across 3,000 miles of open ocean.

After seventeen years of circumnavigation I found myself battling a heart attack. When that battle was won, I came across an ancient little 25-footer to tootle about in as I rebuilt my shattered spirit. She was named, of course, *Heartfelt*. Like a kid,

I still giggle a bit inside when I toy with the conceits of *Unlikely* and *Heartfelt*.

Our boats' names are our secret dreams of childhood. A Russian friend who grew up on the cold steppes of Siberia named his first boat *Arizona* . . . he could imagine no place warmer and no place more unlike Siberia. Or the unself-consciously named *La Forza del Destino* . . . a name only a kid could dream up. Or the surgeon who couldn't avoid the truth and named his boat *Elective Surgery*.

In the end it's not the large events in our lives from which we derive the most coin of pleasure. The big stuff that happens has too much chance, is too stochastic, for us to claim credit honestly. It's the small events for which we can honestly claim kudos that evoke the largest emotional response. Like a child who will find endless joy in a pile of sand on a beach, the old sailor must find his reward in the pure pleasure of smallish events. Like a child experiencing an emotional swing from tearful scary to awe to pure and unrestrained euphoric laughter, the sailor too can allow release of all his hidden, inner self, exposed only to a beloved shipmate and insulated from the judgmental crescendos of the too-crowded land.

At sea a venerable sailor's freedom is a child's freedom: unrestricted, untrammeled, and involved only in the immediate and encompassing events of sailing itself. The universe in a child's eyes is the far reaches of a sandbox. The old sailor's universe isn't much farther than that of a sandbox, reaching only to the three-mile circle of his horizon. The sandbox and the sailing circle, of which the child and the ancient are the undisputed masters, encompass all happiness, unlimited by the dispiriting events that lie beyond their borders.

A small universe, perhaps, but absolutely your own and quite enough to return the largest joys, as Moitessier well knew.

Get Thee in Harm's Way

Sometimes it's damned difficult to find convincing reasons that favor getting old. It's easy to rattle off a litany of the woes of age, but when it comes time to argue its advantages, we slither along the slippery verge of logic.

Being old does have a few evident advantages, and being an old *sailor* beats all, since old salts' sea tales, true or stretched, can put the landbound in awe of you.

The outrageous conceit of sailing a small boat across a big ocean sucks in the attention of nonsailors like a black hole eating stars. Being in thirty feet of sailboat a thousand miles from land is an experience so far beyond the listener's ken that the decades between teller and listener melt away. The rapture grows behind young eyes as you retail the passions of passage. You're no longer an obsolete relic. Instead, you're transmogrified in *their* minds to what you picture in *your* mind you really are: thirtysomething, lithe, tanned, sexy, and full of derring-do.

The process is a cross-pollination of desires. Your desire is to be as young as you really know you are, and their secret desire, which they hope for but never expect to fulfill, is to sail the great oceans. A relationship transpires sans confrontation and with no losers. Both sides sidle up to their innermost itch, one to relive their youth and the other to fill their secret hearts with adventure.

When ordinary old folk put their senescent two cents into conversations, the daunting glaze of boredom often spreads around the table like a Los Angeles smog. Some polite progeny might still retain respect enough to wait out painfully what, admittedly and for the most part, would be unhelpful comments and at worst out-of-touch senile foolishness. More likely the table will simply elide elder comments as if with an aural red pencil, and in doing so effectively elide the elder.

When the world didn't change too much, old folks' observations were germane, helpful, and even interesting. But in our hurtling-forward world of today, yesterday's observations about the current state of affairs sound obsolete in hours. Talk to a younger generation and your listeners might not even understand the language.

Except . . . if the old guy has trod paths of living that the young never will. These paths are damned hard to find since most of whatever you did in your youth the young now do better—been there and have a T-shirt to prove it. But there are arcane pursuits whose relevance cannot be questioned by the young. It is in these rare disciplines, few as they are, that relevance resides for the old and causes the world to retain its curiosity about you.

A sailing history of the great oceans has a peachiness about it that will zing your listeners. Because your adventures are so far afield of their experience, they can't add to it, subtract from it, cast doubt on it, or do damn-all to upstage you. Their job is to listen . . . a condition close to heaven for a gabby old salt. You've got them by the shorts.

As the world gets smaller and as time and distance vanish in the exhaust of jet planes, the mystery and appeal of doing a crossing in a month that the jets do in a few hours becomes one of the last secret lairs of romance in a world where romance is scarce and sorely missed.

It's hard to think of other pursuits in which an old guy can involve himself that, like ocean sailing, can leave listeners on the shore gasping for more. There is almost nothing else that so instructs the know-it-alls that there are adventures undreamed of in their philosophies. Perhaps the astronauts can go on for decades retailing adventures that the generations antecedent can never experience. And also perhaps those few hardy fools who challenge the Himalayas and live to tell about it. And perhaps aquanauts, like Jacques Cousteau, who create untrammeled worlds in which to wander. Perhaps these fortunate few will always have bevies of lubricious lasses and phalanxes of dreaming lads yearning to run into someone who, like yourself, has done the undoable.

Slay dragons, go east as the world goes west, put yourself in harm's way, hold unpopular opinions loudly, and always seek an opportunity to tug at the tail of the tiger. At your great age you have little to lose. You gain the admiration of the world while they acknowledge your audacity.

After some decades of living, no matter how successful, how relevant, how involved you've been in the world, you reach that terrible moment when you can no longer maintain the fiction of being part of that world. Your age conspires to make you a spectator . . . a watcher of the boob tube of history. You're in front of the screen, not on it, and thus you may be condemned to pass some years, even perhaps some decades, realizing that in our swift world the means of involvement are streaming out beyond your reach.

It's not that you're any less than you were . . . indeed, by virtue of your experience-laden years, you're more, much more than you were . . . but the pace has changed, the velocity to keep up is now greased by structures and support systems that are no longer available to you.

You no longer have the time nor the understanding of the new velocities to hold onto even a small piece of the pie. You've fallen under the wagon, and no matter how you clutch at the wheels, you soon fall away.

What to do? It's really screamingly simple. Rather than grabbing at the unclutchable complexity of the "now" in which you live, simplify and set your own standards, your own velocities of a slower, less current wagon, but one in which you have tight control of where you're headed and how fast you want to get there.

It's a matter of rejecting a universe that is rejecting you and of creating a new universe for yourself that fills your needs for involvement. A universe that gives meaning to the last third of your life. A universe in which you're always in the eye of the camera. A universe that's big enough to contain your spirit yet small enough for you to control.

But it must be a heroic universe, a place of derring-do

offering a level of risk that you have long believed you could no longer accept. A place of movement, satisfying velocities, attainable goals, and all, absolutely all, within your control.

For me in my penultimate decades, this universe is my sailing vessel.

Seek out your own.

Where and with Whom

Five

When all goes ill at Sea
And all else fails,

Try being Five.

If that doesn't work,
Nothing will.

HUMPHREY BARTON AND MARY BARTON

Sir Humphrey Barton founded the Ocean Cruising Club in Great Britain. The OCC, unlike other sailing associations, has a membership requirement of a passage of 1,000 miles at sea without touching land. Hum, as he was known to all, and Mary, his wife and sailing mate, crossed the Atlantic in their 27-footer with the ease that most of us exhibit in crossing a street.

Early in his career Hum survived an Atlantic hurricane in which his cabintop was lost in mid Atlantic. He sailed the balance of the crossing as an open boat.

Mary Barton shared many of Hum's later passages. She is, in her own right, a grand old sailor. —Reese

Reese Remembers the Old Admiral

As in chess, a sailing entrance must be elegant, achieved with the least amount of activity, the least amount of fuss, and the fewest possible number of moves. Too much emphasis cannot be placed on this matter of coming into the harbor for, after all, it's the exact goal of our voyage, the end of the entire process of training and of passage that

stretches back over months or years. To begin a long passage well is the sign of a dedicated amateur. To end it well is the sign of an experienced sailor. To become passagemakers we must learn to complete our passage better than we started it lest we be judged by others, and by ourselves, as merely lucky.

A long time ago I was taught my first lesson concerning an elegant entrance. I was emerging from my fiftieth year and sensing the creep of time. I had taken my first tentative steps toward offshore sailing. I was on a chartered sailboat (more boat than sail) in the British Virgins and feeling saltier than a Bismarck herring.

I'd navigated faultlessly and without mishap the entire length of Sir Francis Drake Channel (15 miles). I'd rounded the point of Buck Island without going aground (the depth 20 feet offshore was 100 meters) and had come for the night to the harbor of Tortola.

I made an awful entrance. I took down all sails, fired up the engine, posted crew all over the deck, and sent one poor bewildered soul up the mast as lookout. Neither he nor I was sure about what he was to look out for.

The harbor entrance was wide open, and the boats already anchored were lined up to port of the channel. There was only one buoy in the harbor, warning of a shallow area off a point upon which I promptly went aground. Huffing off the sand, I tangled with someone's anchor rode (fortunately for me it was nylon), and then, with much backing and filling and much roaring of the diesel, I neatly laid my own rode over those of most of the other boats in the harbor. Later that night, needless to say, when all were asleep, including the lad who I should have appointed as anchor watch, I dragged all the way back to the sea wall and took half the harbor with me.

Just after dawn the next morning, exhausted from the entanglements and disentanglements of the night before, I lay on deck and watched a neat Vertue 25 slip silently into harbor. I realized, with horror, that she was without power, but before I could cry havoc and rouse my neighbors to the danger they faced, my attention was caught by the dainty boat ballet to which I had become a privileged audience.

The Vertue came in under full sail, with no engine and no one on the foredeck. Only the helmsman could be seen. The little boat sailed quietly through the cluttered pack, sailing her way among the lumbering charters, and swung around sharply into the wind in a small clear area far from the herd. She stopped dead, much to my landlubberly surprise, as a sailboat must when brought into the wind. The helmsman crawled creakily out of the cockpit and, in an old man's hobble, limped to the bow where his rode had already been flaked out. He silently paid out and put his hook into the harbor bottom. He slowly (for he was a very old man and could do little quickly) took down his main and bagged his jib while the Vertue was finding her natural lay at anchor. He then went aft and disappeared below, from which he reappeared after eight hours, refreshed by a sound nap, as he told me later. The whole process took about ten minutes and was accomplished without a sound.

From this little dance, a soft-shoe shuffle by an old man approaching his eighties, I learned that an entrance into the harbor need not be—nay, must not be—achieved in the shrill tones of panic and dismay. The old man knew his boat, knew her habits, knew the harbor, and had carefully prepared for anchoring. All went as well for him as it had gone badly for me, and not being as dumb as I look, I decided to stop charging full ahead and to start learning. The elegant Ancient Mariner was Sir Humphrey Barton, founder and admiral of the Ocean Cruising Club, Crosser of Big Oceans in Small Vertues. The Admiral had something I wanted.

From this beginning I ultimately learned that a good entrance into any port is no accident. It's a product of thought, judgment, and experience. "An elegant entrance," the Admiral told me, "is when you arrive with the least possible effort, and," he added with a wry smile, "a perfectly elegant entrance is when you do it with no effort at all."

Mary's Thoughts on Sailing with Hum

In 1975, when Hum had made his twentieth Atlantic crossing, and I had no ambition to catch up with him, we decided to make Malta a winter base and to cruise in the Eastern Mediterranean during the summer months.

This was a mistake as there was insufficient challenge
in the Mediterranean. We also found sailing in that sea
to be frustrating as compared with the Atlantic and the
Caribbean.

Advancing age made little real difference: we may have
taken our cruising in gentler and less ambitious fashion, but
never to the extent of sailing our lovely *Rose Rambler* inef-
ficiently. Also, at whatever age, cruising is a way of life, with
every aspect of that life, be it planning, decisions, tasks onboard, moments of delight or disquiet, being more closely
shared than is often the case when living ashore.

—*Mary Barton, 2002*

Sailing Goals

The choice of sailing goals for Ancient Mariners rests on the immutable fact that we old folk have lost the sense of infinite time available that's so characteristic of the young. Our future is foreshortened, and whatever choices we make should fit a tightly constrained time frame that seems sensible and doable.

When I was a young man, my circumnavigation was the gift of a cornucopia of time. In fact, it took eighteen years to get back home. Now, at eighty-plus, I still yearn for at least one more important passage, but time and health instruct that demands on my capacities be modest.

Starting out at sixty or seventy on a global circumnavigation is an act of high hubris. And indeed, sailing around the world does not give much more joie de vivre than a more modest and infinitely more doable transit across the Atlantic. Not all sexagenarians and septuagenarians are emotionally or physically up to an Atlantic crossing, but many have done so. An Atlantic circumnavigation, for those capable, west to east and east to west, can take less than six months. A world circumnavigation can take years and give rise to unimagined, unpredictable confrontations.

Half a year, at our age, is predictable. The sense of accomplishment in spending ever more precious time to complete an ocean passage, whether it be the ambitious transit of the Atlantic or a six-day jaunt to Bermuda, is, for me at least, like nothing else that could be imagined. Sea passages, on one's own bottom, in concert with the universe, reinvent in the old sailor the blood-rushing thrill of simply being alive.

In reality, a passage to and from Europe for even the more decrepit among us is without serious problems so long as we have a good boat that has been well prepared and, most importantly, we choose the only times for which there are no serious weather threats.

Here is your itinerary.

Leave the U.S. East Coast on June 1. Leave from north of

Morehead City, North Carolina, to get the most out of fair winds and the Gulf Stream. There should be no North Atlantic winter gales at this time, although squalls can pop up at any time. Reef early, very early, and squalls are no problem.

Head right out toward Bermuda. It's generally a piece of cake, and you should make port in Bermuda in six days or less. Bermuda becomes a shakedown cruise, and all of the problems that might arise can be handled by the superb marine facilities of that blessedly English-speaking island.

This is the first leg of an Atlantic circumnavigation, but it's sufficient to infuse the old sailor with new life. Not much more will be gained by the next six months that it will take to get back home via the more southerly route, but some, like the climbers of great mountains, will do it simply because it's there.

For those with the time and the strength to proceed, take off as soon as possible for the Azores, a couple of thousand miles to the east. Keep a weather eye to the South Atlantic and the Caribbean, as there is always the minimal possibility of an early hurricane generating in that area. Even if one should occur, it would probably be no serious threat by the time it might get to you in your passage eastward. In my first passage to the Azores we caught the tail end of a hurricane. Gloomy skies, modestly elevated winds, and wonderful long smooth mountains of distant storm-generated seas.

The passage was no problem for this first-time ocean sailor in a slow 32-foot Westsail, and we made the Azores in under twenty days. That passage still remains the high point of my sailing life. The exaltation, the sense of fulfillment, and the pure pleasure of "having done it" was never to be exceeded in my next twenty years at sea. We painted our required picture on the Great Wall of Faial and considered our next leg.

You now have about half a year before the winds and weather become amenable to return along the southerly route. Don't get involved in Europe or the Mediterranean. The presence there of too many other ships and a million officious and objectionable functionaries makes for messy and stressful sailing. The empty sea is much more fun.

Sail south and put up in any of the string of islands that bejewel the African coast. Don't make landfall anywhere in Africa. Some pretty good marine facilities can be found on Las Palmas in the Canary Islands. Time your departure from the Cape Verdes toward the west sometime at the end of December or the beginning of January to catch the Christmas winds.

This becomes the easiest part the passage. With 15 knots blowing steadily and unceasingly off your starboard quarter, all you need to do is set your sails, put your feet up, and wait until you raise Charlotte Point on Antigua. Then it's into English Harbour, where all the dreams of Caribbean adventures come true.

That's it, my old friends. Around the Atlantic basin on your own bottom, by your own ancient brain and muscle in half a year. It will add swagger to your stride and a decade to your life.

For those of you who have chosen passage to and from Bermuda, the sense of accomplishment and of your own self-worth is not a whit demeaned by this more reasonable passage. Indeed, for the more cautious, this piece of the Atlantic can be crossed conjoined with a hundred other yachts in a leisurely race cum cruise that's organized every couple of years.

Whether you do 6,000 miles around the Atlantic or what's essentially an extended day sail to Bermuda, whether you set sail for forty days across the broad Pacific, or indeed whether you merely push off for a breezy afternoon in your own home waters counts little in the emotional content of the act. In all you have accepted the final responsibility for your own safety and survival. Perhaps only here are you truly the master of your soul.

Crew for an Old Skipper

As we advance in years, the selection of crew becomes ever more crucial. We'll be more dependent on others, especially in emergencies and most especially in crises that last more than a few moments. Experienced old sailors can and do respond quickly to an impending threat that can be overcome quickly. Since our reserves are obviously not what they used to be, we tend to forget we're no longer the deck apes we were in decades past. Overlooking a careful assessment of our *present* physical abilities, made rosy by the faulty memory of our energetic past, is downright dangerous. Old folk, holding tight to our youth, tend not to acknowledge limitations. A young skipper can substitute his own energies if his chosen crew turns out inadequate. An old skipper can't afford that eventuality.

An additional problem that's generic in all but the most saintly of septuagenarians and octogenarians is that we tend to be cranky, set in our ways, and generally unreceptive to new ideas or new ways of doing things. In selecting his crew the old skipper must accept the fact that a good deal of the responsibility for unpleasantness that may arise can be due to the grittiness of aging. On the whole, we aren't as nice and as forgiving as we once were. We're certainly not inclined to easily accept advice from callow youth who just may have something really interesting to pass on. We must guard against the insidious hubris of age.

An acceptable crew is a vital part of your offshore adventure. It's unlikely that the sea itself will kill you, but it's very likely that a sour, petulant, and lazy watchmate can make you wish that you were dead. After Elysian visions of passage, a belching, farting, snoring, lazy lout in the next bunk can turn dreams to dross. Trial passages tell you no more about the evil that lurks in the heart of crew than does your first impression. The bad stuff in them, and the good stuff also, appears, as if on schedule, five days out and 500 miles downwind. Taking on crew carelessly is like marrying in haste. It can be followed by long periods of repentance.

Every crew member comes with a bundle of emotional problems, an aeolian box of miseries that you'll get to open when it's too late to do anything about it. Since it hasn't been established that any one human being is really any better or any worse than any other, the only way to deal with crew is to admit that they're as bad as you are. Once admitted, then you can deal with their foibles with as much forgiveness as you deal with your own. Since you haven't been able to change yourself very much in all the years that you've known you, it's unlikely that you'll be able to accomplish much reform on another person inside of the month or so that you'll be together.

Before you get down to the business of acquiring crew, you must be most excruciatingly clear about the financial arrangements with them. If you're an old skipper you're assumed to be rich, for in their minds who else could afford a crewed sailboat. Beware.

There are three ways to go, financially speaking. Paid crew, unpaid crew, and paying crew. All arrangements are full of problems, but the only alternative is to sail alone. Solo sailors, of which there are many more old-timers than young-timers, maintain that they indulge in this lonely form of madness to avoid the madness of dealing with crew.

If you go with paid crew you may expect more of them than with unpaid crew, not because you're paying them, but because they're committed to the sea. If both you and your paid crew are competent, there may be a trial of wills that, if not set right, can unsettle the passage. There can be only one skipper, and that must be you. But though you may be set in your old ways, you must always be flexible enough to at least consider other opinions.

Unpaid crew who will sail with you for found alone tend to be your emotional peers. They're out there for the adventure, the same as you are. Unpaid crew can be drawn from a larger sample than any other, thus making it a bit more likely to match your needs and prejudices. They are, however, considerably less permanent, less reliable, and more likely to jump ship than paid crew.

Then there are crew who will pay you for the privilege of sailing. I've never known a good outcome from taking paying crew aboard. I once witnessed the arrival of a boat in the harbor of Galle in Sri Lanka. The anchor was no sooner in the water than the crew, all paying their way, erupted from the boat like fish scattering from a shark in their haste to be away. The divergence of the stories of the passage, from the venerable skipper on one side and the crew on the other, would have been hilarious had the tellers not been in such emotional pain. Most of the complaints from the old skipper were about a gluttonous, disobeying crew, and those from the crew were about a miserly old skinflint who was parsimonious, demanding, and unkind.

In the long run, accidental acquisition of crew is probably the best way to recruit. Cyndee did a bikini bounce down the dock in Panama and asked, all in one deep breath, if we were "going to Tahiti and could she come along." All male chemicals aboard agreed without investigation or reservation. She came on board sans experience, sans reference, sans everything save a bosun's knife, bubbly enthusiasm, and a bikini. She remained for five years, married my first mate, and left with all of us passionately in love, not only with her figure but with the strength and the consistency of her spirit.

It was a high risk with a happy ending. I have tried vibrating to my hormones on other occasions, rarely with such marvelous luck. Since my hormones, and yours, no longer vibrate as resoundingly as in the past, we may be deprived of a wonderful experience, but more likely we're saved from distress.

On the whole, accidental acquisition is not a bad way to go. Most folk are fundamentally the same, so what you stumble over as you blindly grope about for crew is likely to be as good as what you might agonize over.

Recruiting from among old friends is very, very dangerous. The guy with whom you've pleasantly played poker for years may have an *idée fixe* concerning the nature of your relationship that simply won't work at sea. The nifty gal liked by all may find that close confines and limited social contacts are different than being part of a larger crowd. It's better, far better, to develop a new relationship with crew at sea than to try to transmigrate to your boat relationships that have worked, perhaps for even decades, on land.

And that caution goes for blind hiring, too. In spades! I once hired a sailor sight unseen upon the recommendation of a respected friend. I was in Africa and needed crew to make the passage home. Since there's no crew in Africa and since the praise ("The best sailor I've ever known") sounded great, I sent the stranger a ticket. As it turned out I should have sent two tickets since he took up two seats in the plane. I pictured his 320 pounds on my little 32-footer and quickly conjured up a reason to send him back home.

In the case of this fat man my instinctual repugnance, call it prejudice if you will, had demonstrable validity, as is often the case. A few years later, on a quiet day's sail in protected waters, he fell overboard from someone else's boat, and because those on board were unable to deal with his enormous bulk, he drowned. When I sent him home from Africa I didn't have so specific or horrendous a scenario in mind. He just made me very uncomfortable. The moral? As ever, don't denigrate your feelings, especially since they've been salted by decades of experience.

Should you find crew members whom you really like but whose skills and experience are limited, take them on and teach them. Teaching is, anyway, a function desirable in old skippers. You can't change personality, but you can share knowledge gained from your long and active life. In the final analysis a quieting, or disquieting, feeling in your belly is as good a bellwether as anything.

Abjure smokers, dopers, and alcoholics. While many of your friends on land have habits that may amuse you or at least not repel you, contiguity and time ratchets up repugnance. Dope and alcohol are dangerous magnifiers of irrationality, with which you can do without on a small sailboat. Tobacco, even someone else's tobacco, can ruin your lungs and stink up your boat.

Choosing and Living with Your Choice

Having avoided smokers, dopers, and drunks, we must live with the choices that we've made. Any attempt we may make to seriously change how a person acts and reacts is feckless and unrewarding. In our own egregious habits, we find it difficult to change. Why, then, should we have expectations that others, neither better nor worse than ourselves, can change their ways of living for the sake of a sea passage. We're all made up of bundles of traits, some "good" and some "bad." Some traits are more acceptable to a skipper choosing a crew, and some traits are less acceptable. There can be no perfect crew, so there will be no perfect choice. At best, your crew won't be more perfect than you are. Your approval of crew that you've chosen is the ultimate method of assuring good passages. Disapproval always returns disapproval. Approval never does.

While there exist ancient and accurate charts of the sea that tell in exquisite detail what you may expect in all the great oceans, there still do not exist any guidelines to determine whether the sailing crew you're signing on are devils or angels.

In truth, you don't want either. Too good can be as exasperating as too bad. What's needed on a small boat over a long passage is someone whose faults are mildly attractive and whose good qualities don't cause your own ancient habits and prejudices to suffer by comparison.

A Bestiary for Old Sailors

By whatever standards you may wish to apply, dogs as crew are better than people. They never judge you by your age. To your dog, you're eternal. Because dogs seem to sense debility, and the older you are, the more they love you, and the more they yearn to help.

Dogs rarely talk (a relief on a small boat) and almost never have an opinion on sail trim that differs from your own. They're silent and most congenial crewmates. And so are cats and birds and monkeys and anything else that has the blessed inability to speak.

That doesn't mean that they're not good listeners. They're superb listeners and will lie at your feet drinking it all in for as long as you wish to tell yet again tales of youthful derring-do and half-mythic recounting of loves lost. Even after a month or so, when the more lingual crew has been known to throw themselves over the side rather than listen once more to your tales of amatory adventures, your dog will even pant a little as you get to the juicier bits.

Cats seem not to be as good listeners since they have the talent to do other things while being regaled. Cats will either sleep or lick themselves, both of which activities are likely to suggest that you're not getting their entire attention. However, a purr at the right moment is sometimes as good as a pant.

Of the entire zoological spectrum available as crew, all are, in their own way, equally delightful to be with. Some, like the pig, may be a bit too equal, and some, like the horse, may not fit the forecastle. But from among all God's creatures who are reasonably sized, there's certainly more than one silent, adoring, and nondemanding animal who will more perfectly fit your own ancient, set-in-concrete, idiosyncratic profile than will any human. Whatever the animal is, it will demonstrate a loyalty that will make the grudging acquiescence of crew and, indeed, family seem mutinous by comparison.

For sailors with a practical turn of mind there are birds.

Hens are nice because they supply eggs. A brace of pigeons of the homing variety will bring help if you can stay afloat long enough for them to get home. A pelican, whose bill can hold more than his belly can, might be signed on for his skill as a fisherman. A ribbon tied loosely around the pelican's neck will prevent fish in his bill from becoming fish in his belly. A bit unfair, perhaps, but the pelican will love you nonetheless for it. Try that on a two-legged crew and see what happens.

The trouble with birds is that, perhaps due to their saurian precedents, they lack (lovebirds notwithstanding) demonstrative affection. Since affection is the chief reason (next to having a permanent auditor) for carrying pets aboard in the first place, perhaps you should try an unfeathered genus.

Snakes immediately head for the bilge, from which you can rarely entice them out for a chat, and holding a conversation with your bilge is liable to panic your crew. Turtles are dull, and although a pet rat is nice, you would probably have to choose between it and your wife.

From among the vast bestiary available to voluble Ancient Mariners as taciturn crew, it all comes down to man's best listener, the dog. True, dogs do have a few habits that can't be trained out of them. Some tend to be a bit flatulent (but so are you, you old fart), and some drool too enthusiastically when showing affection (but so do you). Some dogs, as they age, will tend to nod off in mid-listen, but that certainly sounds familiar. Others shed hair about the boat, and some may be a bit too jealous, but all in all, dogs as crew are the best beasts.

In addition to scratching your lonely bone, dogs serve serious purposes aboard a small boat. They are the watch that never sleeps when you, approaching well-earned dotage, tend to nod off. They will, in port, loudly announce the approach of friend or foe. Any dog bigger than a bread box is sufficient to dissuade strangers when you're aboard, and they'll alert the neighborhood should you be ashore. They will defend you to the death and will defend your ladies' honor even, unfortunately, sometimes against you.

A major consideration is that all zoological crew are restricted by the exclusionary health laws of nations that seem intent on keeping them out. Paradoxically, the most rigid by far is England, that country of animal huggers who, on one hand, consider that vivisecting an animal vivisectionist is a boon, not a crime, and who, on the other hand, will ban your beast at their border. In spite of England's love for animals, regulations require that your perfectly healthy mutt must languish for lonely months in quarantine awaiting the improbable bloom of some *canis arcanus* disease. Other nations are almost as strict, so that it's possible that your 200-pound mastiff may never be allowed off your only slightly heavier boat. Should you opt for a large dog, make it a water spaniel or some other breed that will get its exercise in the water and won't yearn after forbidden beaches.

Some countries are reasonable about quarantining animals, and after you're in port for a while, officials seem to forget their legal passion for canine rejection. As ever, a little baksheesh helps.

Disposal of doggy-do is no problem since dogs are easily trained to "do" in a delegated place at a delegated time. Even an old dog can be taught this new trick, and a pup is a cinch. The only thing you cannot teach a dog to do is hang his heinie over the rail, and in all fairness, I don't know many sailors who have mastered that technique, either. At any rate, don't let the small problem of personal pup hygiene deny you the pleasure of having a dog aboard, especially since he would rather be with you than anywhere else in creation.

One thing that you don't have to worry about is doggy mal de mer. Animals seem not to get seasick, but when they do, or if they do, it's usually characterized by a need for lots of sleep. If you happen to own a lazy dog to begin with, you may wonder if he's feeling a bit dizzy or just running true to breed. With a naturally nappy pussy cat you'll never know.

One personal experience with an animal was memorable and, though bittersweet, delicious. We were enjoying the effusive Japanese hospitality of the Kansai Yacht Club near Kobe when a sorry, sick, and bedraggled kitten wandered aboard.

Our human crew immediately degenerated into sentimental wrecks, and for three days we fed, ministered to, and monitored that poor tyke until she quietly, like the lady she was, gave up her little ghost. We found a small rise at the sea's edge where we buried her. She'd been with us only three days, and beast though she was, she gave us the most human of all our moments of passage.

By all means take an animal as crew. They are, perhaps, God's apology for all the human misfits in the world.

The Old New Breed

Not until the Second World War came to its panting halt was it possible for any but the youngest and strongest of folk to approach sailing as a source of gratification. The racing of boats, which supplies its own bizarre gratifications, rarely having to do with taking pleasure of the sea, has been around longer than our century. The origin of racing lies in commercial competition: who could get to the fish "fustest with the mostest," and never mind the misery for the crew. The tea clippers, in their epic, competing passages to and from the Indies, and their sister ships, which rounded the Horn or landmarched across the Isthmus, all had to do with the incestuous equation by which time and money are related. The faster . . . the more profit to owners. The faster . . . the more agony and danger to crew.

With the advent of fiberglass, reasonably reliable electronics, Dacron sails and sheets, nylon line, and stainless steel, the sailing world changed dramatically. People, especially old folk, could, for the first time in history, make the argument that sailing can be fun.

Those of us who go to sea know that venturing out in a small boat is hardly *fun* in the accepted meaning of the word. For young or old sailors, committing oneself to wind and wave is scary, cold, wet, nauseating, and even a little dangerous now and then. But we do it, and some of us keep doing it beyond our eighties, so sailors must have found some pleasure beyond all that pain.

The human psyche is such that what's reasonably possible becomes compulsively doable, and what's doable with risk and pain, to many, becomes a paradoxical source of pleasure. It's this yearning for frightening, challenging pleasure that drives thousands of retirees to sell the ranch, learn port from starboard, and venture out to the sea. These folk know, beyond any logic, that they simply must get onto a boat. Fantasy, image, and reality come together like an orgasm the first time that their sailboat takes a bone in her teeth, bans boredom, and brings high adventure into old lives.

It's not only the sea that calls; at an age when we old folk are often relegated to back of the bus, still being able to amaze others while pleasuring ourselves is a pretty nifty feeling.

It's an unarguably good thing that happens when large numbers of folk involve themselves in an activity in which, if there's a risk, it's only to themselves and not to our fragile eco-sphere. It's also rare that any gratifying activity is as unlikely to impose on the rights and freedoms of our neighbors as is sailing. Sailing is a private matter between you and the sea or, if you're still so inclined, between you and your god. It's an activity that costs the Earth a mere scintilla of resources compared to the voluminous return of delights. Sailors use up nothing; they pass the natural world along to the next generation as they found it . . . a pretty thought that would look good carved on anyone's stone.

It's especially salubrious for old folk to find a pursuit that will preserve meaning and relevance. Being full of years, I'm selfishly fond of the fact that sailing has almost no upper age limit. Nothing has to be done quickly on a sailboat, and rarely is great strength needed. Should immoderate muscle be required, it's usually in circumstances where the sea would overcome the strongest of us. Old farts and deck apes alike, compared to the physics of the sea, are reduced to essential equality. And how nice to have a physical activity in which you're a hero in the eyes of your grandchildren.

We old salts take pleasure and give no pain in an activity that becomes, as the decades progress, less and less dangerous. "Full fathom five my father lies" is heard now only from bearded guitarists and rarely from bereaved children. Sailing is no longer a sentence . . . nay, it is, instead, a welcome reprieve from the confines of rest homes and importunate clamors of land.

This new species of old-sailors-for-pleasure, so recently aborning, already is dividing in two breeds. On which side of the line you fall depends on the subtle question of how you take your pleasure.

If you take your delight in achieving goals, getting to places at which you directed your vessel, and getting there in quick time and high éclat, then you're the direct descendent of all those iron men who sailed the seas for profit and glory. The game's in the getting there. The delights of a new land are your attraction, and getting there smartly on your own bottom is your reward.

But if the game for you is in the doing, and if you hunger not after the port just ahead and miss not the port just abandoned, then you're heir to no steely antecedents. You are, my friend, an entirely new breed who revels not in the getting to anyplace but in the pure unadulterated glory of simply doing sailing. You're a passagemaker, a sailor to whom the sublimity is being out there in unhampered commune with nature and self. You're a process sailor to whom the act of passing across a hundred miles of water is sufficient for the day. You never say *to* anywhere; rather, you always say *toward* somewhere. You never have a time you must be at a place . . . your place to be is the open sea itself.

You'll likely make long passages, never having planned to sail further than Bimini, and you may, as I did, sail around the world quite by accident.

I applaud those driven folk who must make this port or that in this time or that, since I applaud all sailors.

But I choose the wanderers, the aimless ones, the Moitessiers, as my friends.

Outfitting the Ancient Mariner

Uncounted Years

God looked down one day to see
A curious ship on a glorious sea.

"My God (that's Me) by Jesus," quoth He,
"Mine eyes have seen the glory of Me.

"What I see is more glory for Me—
A Sailor gliding on my shining Sea.

"So caring is he
Of the nature of Me
I'll not take away years he
Spends at Sea."

Ted Brewer designed Unlikely VII *for me in 1979. We sailed her for twenty years, took her around the world (or she took us), and never had a bad moment with her. Ted Brewer's designs seem to be invented for Ancient Mariners. His boats are sea kindly . . . willing to give up a quarter of a knot of speed in trade for safety and comfort.*

Thanks, Ted.

—Reese

Ted Brewer on Simplicity

As I grow older I become more and more convinced that the KISS principle ("Keep It Simple, Stupid") is the way to go and that a simple ship is a happy ship.

I also like Chapelle's statement that exposed plumbing is seaman-like. I'd add exposed wiring to that because Murphy's law prevails at sea. Best to be able to get to stuff fast.

When I designed *Unlikely*, I put in an old-fashioned sea chest so that one through-hull stops *all* incoming water. I'm gratified to hear from you that this simple addition kept *Unlikely* from sinking in the Red Sea.

—*Ted Brewer, 2002*

So many wonderful things happen by purest chance. As I laid out the plot for this book I started my search for old sailors who, by their continuing love for the sea, teach us all what we should be doing with our "declining years." I spread my net widely around the globe only to find that my neighbor just across the canal in Key West was the perfect paradigm for the argument of this book.

All hail to Fred Schwall, who survived a Japanese prison camp and continues, in his eighties, along with his wife of similar age, to survive daily sorties into the Gulf Stream.

—Reese

Fred Schwall on Preparation

As a still sailing old sailor whose eightieth birthday was in 2002, I've found that sailing is still fun and doable for my wife and me by following the usual safety rules a little more closely and cautiously than we might have done in our younger years.

Preparation is the key word. First preservation of ourselves and second of our vessel.

Keeping our bodies in condition for sailing is more difficult, but it's doable with a more stringent exercise program and diet watch—less booze and fast foods and more sleep seem to help us. Daysailing often with short trips to an overnight anchorage in a nice protected cove also helps and mirrors our more ambitious passages.

Attitude is of prime importance.

The difficult part of being an older sailor is admitting to ourselves that those long, wet, windy, rough, and sometimes frightening days at sea aren't what we need to be doing. We bruise and break easier and heal slower than we did in earlier years. We should no longer feel the need to prove ourselves by challenging the sea and the weather except on our conditions of comfort at sea. In other words, a few more days visiting in coward's cove waiting for a really good weather window is OK.

Make your movements slower and more deliberate and thought out—one hand for the boat, the other hand and both feet for you!

Preparing our vessel so there's no need to go forward on the deck in heavy weather is important—lead those lines aft into the cockpit for sail control. Install and use those davits to move the dingy, the outboard engine, and other objects that seem to have become heavier in the last few years.

We, my wife Jean and I, commissioned our 33-foot Hunter the *Sea Tiger* in Key West, Florida, in September 1980, and we've enjoyed putting more than 23,000 miles on the log. We've personally done nearly all repairs and maintenance on her in the past twenty plus years. *Sea Tiger* is aptly named, for I was one of General Chenault's (of Flying Tiger Fame) forgotten warriors in the China-India-Burma Theater during World War II.

—*Fred K. Schwall, Maj. USAF Ret., 2002*

What to Sail

There's a lovely tale about the first fully automated passenger flight. After the plane was airborne, the cabin loudspeaker informed the passengers that "Everything is working perfectly and nothing can go wrong . . . nothing can go wrong . . . nothing can go wrong . . ."

The fact is that, as system complexity increases arithmetically, failure rates increase exponentially. With his own old frame demonstrating a few annoying failures, the Ancient Mariner should seek simplicity in his life, diet, habits, and, most importantly, the boat he chooses to carry him reasonably forward into the decades after sixty.

In my own experience I roamed the world in a 46-foot Ted Brewer one-off. While I was doing the passages the adventure seemed sensible and reasonable even though the circumnavigation was made between the ages of fifty and seventy. In hindsight, however, as I peer down now from a very mature eighty, it astounds me that I had the temerity to take a 22-ton sailboat, with its attendant complexity, into Third World seas.

Now I know better. Now, contemplating my next, and perhaps my final, passages, I'm forced to match my ever more limiting resources, physical and financial, with a boat that will not overwhelm me.

Here are a few observations.

Complexity

When NASA was designing their early space flights they invented a marvelous, technologically complex ballpoint pen that would write in space and only cost a skillion dollars. The Russians used a pencil.

Length of Passage

Come to the realization, as I have, that there are no more circumnavigations and perhaps even no more blue-water passages except for the most spry among us. You and I should both be sailing within a reasonable, one-week circle. Sailing 250 miles out and 250 miles back seems about right unless, as mentioned earlier (pages 32–33), you have the temerity and the strength to do a Bermuda passage. We also allow an Atlantic circumnavigation for those precious few who are bearers of exceptional genes of longevity associated with genes that carelessly denigrate risk.

You must make a choice: 180 days around the Atlantic, two weeks to and from Bermuda, or, for most of us, half a week or less of daysailing. This becomes a complicated decision based on personal physical and emotional factors.

For daysailing or for 250 miles, almost any size sailing vessel will do. A boat 27 feet to 38 feet seems about right. In fact, a good rule of thumb for an old sailor contemplating his future is to knock ten or twenty feet off whatever he's sailing at age sixty. A smaller boat will encourage short and satisfying passages that the effort needed to sail a bigger boat will discourage. You'll sail more, although for shorter periods. This seems to me to be an excellent and sensible doff of the hat to old bones.

Sail Plan

If you're sailing a yawl or ketch rig, seek out the much simpler sloop (single-mast) rig. One or two fewer sails can make an enormous difference. Be aware, however, that a single mast will carry a somewhat larger mainsail. Everything, as in life itself, is a compromise.

Keel Shape

You shouldn't seek speed. Speed under sail is only for obsessed racers for whom an additional quarter of a knot is sought at any expense. Your progress should be stately, as befits your age, so avoid spade keels. They might make you go a bit faster, but they'll add unacceptable discomfort to your aged frame. Acquire, instead, a nice long keel, with lots of wetted surface that will grip the sea and keep you from going too much to lee. Being sea kindly, a long comfortable keel will preserve you to sail another day.

Dropped keels are only for those folk who simply must go faster downwind and who don't mind, or who are thoughtless of, the additional threat to a vessel that a dropped keel might refuse to drop, refuse to undrop, or, at times, simply drop off.

Engine

My 46-footer was powered by a four-cylinder Perkins, and I was surprised to find that many smaller vessels had the same engine, where it was an unnecessary show of power.

I'll choose a smaller power plant, but I'm secretly ashamed that I couldn't follow my own dream and go the "Pardey way." Lin and Larry Pardey simply sail with no engine and no electronic navigation and seem to have a wonderful time of it. Of course, both of their ages added together are very nearly the same as mine.

Mast and Boom

Opt for a tall aspect rig. This simply means a short boom and less sail area in the noncrucial trailing edge of your main. Less canvas translates into less effort on your old bones, and a short boom reduces the number of times that you get brained on your brittle noggin uncushioned by hair. This one is a no-brainer.

Perhaps the best choice would be an unstayed mast. There's lots less stuff to get snagged, and it's easier on your sails and easier on you. Besides, when a shroud goes, as they do, a stayed mast comes down. This can't happen if your mast is unstayed to begin with.

Hull Material

Steel rusts, wood will break your heart, expensive aluminum electrolyzes, and birch bark is only good for canoes. Another no-brainer. Fiberglass is the least taxing on your limited resources of energy.

Ground Tackle

I can no longer haul a 60-pound plow, and fearing the worst, I switch my electric windlass on with bated breath. I must admit surprise and delight when the plow slides effortlessly up with its 300 feet of heavy chain. I also have three 20-pounders, which give twice the holding power and five times the flexibility. For anchors that creaky old you will be able to handle, the solution is small and many.

If you must use a windlass, see pages 55 and 80.

Boat Age
The age of your replacement boat, in boat years, like dog years, should approximate your own. My choice is for the 1960s to late 1970s, when builders were fearful of the strength of fiberglass so they piled it on. My 46-foot Brewer was delivered in 1980 and shows absolutely no structural signs of aging. My replacement might be a Morgan 38 built ten years earlier.

Repairability
I'm distrustful of any system when I can't immediately understand how it functions. If I can't at least jury-rig a repair with pliers, screwdriver, and bobby pin, then I'll carry a backup.

I've tried to make my observations on your next boat as general as possible. Boats, even perhaps more than wives and husbands, are intensely personal choices. It may be that the boat you choose to sail into your old age will violate all of my suggestions. So be it. So long as it doesn't interfere with the extension of your sailorly life, I'll celebrate your choice.

The bottom line is . . . whatever it takes . . . keep sailing.

Outfitting

From the point of view of those over sixty, the most attractive thing about sailing, either as a sport or as a way of life, is that speed and strength are not central to its enjoyment.

There's nothing that needs to be done on a sailing vessel that can't be done slowly, and with proper mechanical assists, there's no activity that's beyond the capabilities of ancient muscles.

Weight

Notwithstanding, there are peculiar needs of age that can be easily dealt with by the proper selection of equipment. The most important is the problem of weight. Traditionally sailing equipment is overbuilt, which translates into overweight. Lightweight, as in anchors, can easily equal or surpass their heavier brothers. A C.Q.R. plow is twice the weight of a Danforth and in most cases holds as well. The slight advantage that a C.Q.R. provides in grass is not enough to overcome the backbreaking effort required to handle it.

Although the simplest mechanical solution to any problem is best for an old back, take a chance and invest in an electric windlass. *But . . .* make sure that it can be easily operated manually when it malfunctions or when electric power disappears. Power your windlass with a battery mounted in the forepeak, as the voltage drop and the drain on batteries from a long, heavy cable to batteries mounted at a distance is severe.

Rode

While chain is wonderfully secure in any situation, its weight is a terrible burden. However, you must use a long chain tail on the anchor since most abrasion to anchor rode happens on the bottom. To save weight use stainless chain. It's much lighter and doesn't rust, but it's not quite as strong as *new* common steel.

Life Rafts

There's one crucial area in which weight can be not only back-saving but lifesaving as well. The life rafts that are generally offered are of such weight that Paul Bunyan would be required to heft them. A life raft is accessed when stress and danger are high, and the sailor is already exhausted. There's only one product among all those I've tested that works for my old back. The Winslow Life Raft Company produces a cruising raft that weighs only 37 pounds, a mere third of the weight of other brands. There's even a featherweight racing version that weighs in at 31 pounds! In an emergency this can be the difference between life and death when you have to deploy it from a leaping, tortured vessel with the sea at its gunwale.

It comes in a small canvas bag for which we built a home in one of our cockpit hatches. We timed how long it would take us to get the raft out of the hatch, out of its bag, and overboard and clocked in at less than forty-five seconds.

Navigation

If you have a chip of wood and any old watch, you have a chip log with which you can time your speed through water with great accuracy. If you've been sailing for a long time, wind speed is easily estimated, and with ribbons of cotton tied port and starboard to shrouds you can always know the only thing a sailor must always know . . . where the wind is coming from.

We're all tempted by the electronic miracles offered, although they don't, on the whole, offer much functional advantage over ancient techniques. If you go for serious electronics, and you will, be very sure that you buy the simplest available. Davis has a handheld anemometer that works adequately well, and the aforementioned chip of wood will get you across an ocean as handily as a thousand-dollar cousin.

When you go for electronics, don't opt for integrated systems. Each sensor should direct its attention only to its own repeater. Avoid the expensive and delicate onboard computers that manufacturers love to sell. Go *integral* rather than *inte-*

grated. You'll save yourself a bundle and in an emergency be much safer.

Global Positioning System (GPS)

Now we come to GPS. It is impossible to argue against this celestial replacement for the stars. The great boon of GPS is that the lat/long location of harbors, lights, reefs, sunken ships, and drying rocks can all be jammed into a handheld GPS. It behooves the sailor who clings close to the shore and all of these navigational dangers to pay close attention to the GPS. For those who venture farther away, the importance of GPS diminishes with each mile sailed away from shore.

These systems are cheap enough that you can carry two or three. Old salts among you who can still shoot the sun for a noon sight (dead easy) are to be imitated. Young salts should buy a cheap sextant, even plastic will do, and at least learn to get your latitude. With latitude and enough time you can, like Columbus, get anywhere in the world by sailing down latitude lines.

Old sailors should avoid digital color readouts. They're much more expensive, and the additional complication adds one more potential for breakdown. Additionally, we don't see as well as we used to, and the clarity of a black-and-white repeater can never be equaled by the clutter of color. This clarity contributes much relief to old eyes.

The problem is that black-and-white instruments, especially graphic GPS repeaters, are getting scarce. The best of breed is the Garmin 152. It is wonderfully inexpensive, it boasts a blessed black-and-white screen that is easy on old eyes and has the capability to shift from Small Numbers to Big Numbers in a flash. The manual is (unlike some) written in straightforward, simple English. An hour of careful perusal will make any old salt into an electronic genius. Read the manual!

Emergency Position-Indicating Radio Beacon (EPIRB)

There is, unfortunately, no substitute for a 406-megahertz EPIRB (emergency position-indicating radio beacon). When survival is measured in hours rather than in days, as is often the case with old hands with fewer reserves of energy, a 406 EPIRB, which transmits your latitude and longitude to a satellite and then to coastal authorities, can bring help in a matter of minutes. These units, are, however, unreasonably expensive. They can be rented or borrowed, but don't sail anywhere without one (for more on EPIRBs, see page 73). In a recent case a sailor in a 26-footer heading toward Catalina Island, 25 miles off of Los Angeles, was found months later hundreds of miles at sea. With a 406 EPIRB he would have been scooped up in hours.

Charts

As a stubborn old coot, I confess to a love affair with paper charts. Awkward, expensive, and hard to store, they are an irrational solution in the face of products such as Navionics. But charts don't go out of whack, and they need no power to use. Charts such as the Navionics digitals, which we have aboard in spite of my passion for paper, combined with the black-and-white Raymarine repeater, remain, for us, the best choice from the bewildering array of electronic offerings.

Solar

Speaking of electrical power, there's no excuse for any sailor, young or old, not to have a solar source. We installed a kit by Siemans that has flawlessly maintained our batteries for over a year. The system that comes with an automatic regulator is seamless. Hook it up and forget it.

Seasick

Let's face it. We all get seasick. Those who say they don't are either lying or bragging, or they have a serious inner ear anomaly. The medication of choice for a long time has been scopolamine, which is a central nervous system depressant. The problem with scopolamine used for seasickness, for me at least, has been the method of delivery. Scopolamine taken by mouth as pills is something that old sailors should avoid because of its impact on the nervous system. Taken as skin patches, scopolamine has somewhat less impact but is still a fixed dose that can give an ancient nervous system what for.

In my own experience I had to discontinue both methods. The oral method left me drowsy, and the patch method irritated my skin and, because it's an unregulated dosage, also led to drowsiness.

Scopolamine has recently been offered as a tablet under the name Scopace with effectiveness claimed for eight hours. My experience has been that it indeed does work for me over the eight hours. It banishes seasickness and left me alert and in charge of my vessel. All this good stuff despite a warning from the maker that any activity that requires alertness should be avoided.

I don't claim to be a doctor, so by all means confer with your physician. Old sailors should be doubly cautious as old-age debilities, such as prostate and glaucoma problems, are sensitive to the drug. For me it worked like a charm.

Rig Aspect and Unnecessary Sail Area

The worst thing about my beloved *Unlikely* is that it was designed just before the high-aspect rig was developed. As a result I have this enormous, long, clumsy, and heavy boom dancing perilously about. A crack on the noggin is something that doesn't improve an old sailor's day at sea.

The long boom adds greatly to the weight of the main. I asked Ted Brewer whether I could reduce the foot of the main and how much function I would lose. "Not much," he said, so I recut a spare main and shortened the foot, thus instantly converting *Unlikely*'s sail plan to a high-aspect rig. I still have the monster boom swinging about, but with a shortened foot it's much more manageable.

I hardly noticed any difference in performance. Of course, if I were a racer, the loss of canvas would certainly lead to loss of races, but I assume that old sailors have more sense than to abuse their already age-abused bodies by the egregious practice of racing sailing boats.

Wives

The best, unarguably the very best, device to have aboard for an old sailor is a younger wife. Any wife is an asset, as she will coddle and comfort you, cook for you, say "poor baby" a lot, encourage you when you're down, and warm you when the chills set in.

But a younger wife can climb the mast.

Reefing

The only mainsail reefing system that doesn't have the seeds of disaster built into it is jiffy reefing.

The main argument against jiffy reefing is that it requires the sailor to exit the safety of the cockpit to reef, although most jiffy reefing can be accomplished by lines led to the cockpit so the main can be brought down without going forward. If you combine this with lazyjacks, you'll have a truly safe and foolproof reefing system.

Indeed, it's valuable for the sailor to go to forward once in a while even if it's not necessary. You never know what you'll find in a "circumnavigation of your mast."

Headsail reefing of a hanked-on sail can also be accomplished from the cockpit and is much preferred to being dependent on a little drum and the additional strain that roller reefing can put on your headstay. In a hassle with the sea, when your mast is being whipped about, the bare steel of a headstay gives less resistance to the wind and thus is infinitely safer than one with a sail wound around it.

That is, if indeed the sail does get wound correctly. In my experience with a handful of systems, it often doesn't. The window shading that leaves a triangle of sail unwound can lead to the loss of the vessel or, at best, a very nasty problem of control.

Sail Size

The rule is the smaller the better. By all means use a high-aspect rig with a small boom. It saves the crews' heads, and you have much less weight with which to deal. Smaller sails lose only a fractional amount of boat speed, and since you're cruising and not racing, what in damnation is your hurry?

Boomless Staysail

My *Unlikely* came with a boomed staysail. The boom that is self-tending in a weir or a tack has the nasty habit of whacking you on your bottom if you're lucky and on your top if you're not. After sustaining abuse from this devilish device, I called Ted Brewer (I call Ted a lot) and asked if I could remove the boom and if I would lose speed or control if I did so. His laconic answer was, as usual, "Not much." I deep-sixed the boom, and after sailing for two decades without it I've noticed only that I receive fewer bruises.

Mast Rails

Mast rails are a web of steel tubing port and starboard at the base of the mast, usually at waist height, that takes your weight as you work at the mast while your boat leaps about in a heavy sea.

Don't sail without them. Don't sail without them. Don't sail without them. In case the old sailor reading this did not read correctly, I've repeated it the magical three times. A young strong deck ape may very well have the upper body strength to stay himself with that "one hand for the boat," but you and I can't.

Line Size

In selecting line size for an old salt, unlike most of the other recommendations, the larger diameter line is preferred, as it gives well-used and perhaps arthritic hands something upon which to get a good grip. Fat line is both heavy and expensive but won't cut into flesh, and because its girth is amenable to handling, it'll serve better in an emergency.

Outboard Size

We all carry an outboard, but all too often we burden our old backs with a motor of so many horses that the job of getting it on and off is often not worth the trouble on a 9-foot inflatable. Who needs a big engine to get from ship to shore? Anything more powerful than 3.5 horsepower is an abusive luxury. A 10-horse motor will get you ashore sooner . . . but do we really need to worry about saving a minute or two? The small engines have the great advantage of simplicity of operation and ease of repair, and they're easy on the pocketbook. No one really needs a reverse gear or, indeed, any gear. Gears add weight, cost, and complications. And absolutely no one needs an electric start, which compounds the felony with the need to deal with a 12-volt battery. The best choice is the lightest-weight, pull-start motor that can be swiveled around 360 degrees to produce a virtual reverse. Don't worry when others point and snicker . . . you'll be ashore while they're still muscling their monster over the rail.

Diesel Size

Please remember that you're sailing in a vessel that has a displacement hull. Simply stated, that means you can add horsepower till the cows come home, and not a whit will be added to your speed. A displacement hull, at hull speed, digs a hole in the water from which it refuses to emerge. The more horsepower, the deeper the hole. A most feckless endeavor.

Be very modest in your selection of engines. My 46-foot vessel is powered by a 55-horsepower diesel and has been equal to any task set upon it. I've often been surrounded by idiot 10-foot inflatables with outboards of horsepower almost twice mine. What are they thinking?

Waterbox (Sea Chest)

A waterbox provides a single intake of seawater for the entire vessel. It has a single through-hull valve that, when closed, cuts off seawater to all onboard saltwater systems. The lines running into the box from various parts of the boat have their own shut-off valves, allowing you to isolate individual systems.

A young and frisky contortionist is recommended for those terrifying moments when the water is rising and no one is sure from where. The immediate action is to race around the boat, crawl into uncrawlable spaces to get at scattered intakes below the waterline through-hull intakes. If you are not young and not frisky and not a contortionist, you can lose the race with the rising water. The solution is unutterably simple. Install a waterbox that has one through-hull valve for intake and a number of outflow valves coming from it that lead to the inboard water systems. Thus, when in dire straits, or even when leaving the boat unattended for a bit, simply reach down and shut of the single waterbox intake through-hull valve. Instantly your vessel is safe from rising water.

Things That Add Nothing to Your Enjoyment of the Sea
Hot water, refrigeration, and air-conditioning are just three of the "necessities" you can do without. See page 87 for my opinions on these and the rest.

Anti-Furling

Winds howling
Start winding
Furl binding
Sails clanking
Should'a been hanking

The very first thing you're told, young or old, soft sailor or bold, is that you simply must have sails that furl themselves. Sail-makers will furl your jib and your main, and if you're a ketch they'll furl your mizzen (during which they furl your pocket-book).

All you have to do, say the furlers, is stay in your cockpit and, "with little or no effort," shorten sail.

The central problem with all furling gear is that there are trade-offs for the "little or no effort." For a momentary easing of effort you trade off the blessings of long-term simplicity. The high level of engineering required by furling gear generates two things to be avoided.

First, it zooms up the price of your sail-shortening gear. If you're rich (a four-letter word), maybe that's not so important. But the second problem that is endemic in *all* furling gear involves a threat to life, and that *is* important.

I've had two occasions when furling gear (the most expensive that I could buy) threatened the survival of my vessel.

One event almost sank us. A central and seemingly uncorrectable characteristic of all furling gear is what can best be described as window shading, like when you try to wind up a window shade, and it leaves an aggravating piece of blind unwound.

While furling gear works well, more or less, in modest winds, no furling gear can handle high winds. If winds are over 40 or 50 knots, when you crank in your headsail, with enormous effort, it will usually leave a wispy triangle of sail streaming off the headstay. It happened to me, close off the coast of my home port in New Jersey, when a couple of short squalls roared from the west. The little triangle was enough to put us on beam ends, and had my vessel not had a high entrance at the companionway hatch that kept the sea from sloshing below, we would not have been able to save the boat.

Old sailors should go to extreme ends to eliminate all avoidable serious emergencies. The problems inherent in furling gear are avoidable by not using it.

But if you're planning only daysailing with all of the attendant responses to lee shores and shifting winds, on smaller vessels a jib reefing system may well be justified.

My editor, who considered my tilt against roller reefing to be a bit impertinent, wrote me the following note: "Roller reefing may be a needless complication for voyaging but it enabled my father to keep daysailing a few more years." Well said, Redactor. I concede, since underlying *everything* in this book is the bedrock argument that *anything* that extends the sailorly life is to be desired.

For other than pure daysailing in complicated waters there's nothing simpler, easier, or cheaper than hanked-on sails. Halyards can be led to the cockpit, downhauls for jib and mains are cheap to install, and lazyjacks will neatly tuck up and gather in your main until a crisis is resolved.

The effort required to wind in a furling sail in half a gale is daunting, no matter what the furlers say. By comparison, the effort to drop a hanked-on or slide-mounted sail with the proper downhaul is child's play.

Which is, after all, the game that old folk young in heart really want to play.

Anti-Stays

Of the problems that have bedeviled me and threatened my vessel, the most egregious and damaging were those events that involved failures, of one kind or another, of stays or shrouds.

The shrouds and stays of my cutter-rigged sail plan are an ever-present source of danger that requires careful attention, replacement, and maintenance. When my son, some years ago, started preaching the advantages of unstayed masts, I, as fathers are wont to do, pooh-poohed the suggestion. Now, after some thought and three scary events, I pooh him no longer.

We were heading up the Red Sea along the coast of Oman, a very questionable place to be, when a fitting at the masthead of my headstay broke the stay. The rigger who'd put up the stay failed to allow free movement in all directions, and the resulting flexing broke the stainless steel cable. The winds, coming from astern, were kindly, and the mast stayed up.

On another occasion we were heading down the Red Sea off the coast of then-communist Ethiopia when, for no discernible reason, the port shrouds gave way. This time, we lost our mast.

Finally, on the last leg of our circumnavigation, as we headed back across the Atlantic, the headstay, perhaps because it was over five years old, snapped and deposited our jenny into the water and under our hull at 2 a.m. It was a mess that took four of us half a night and day to clean up. We completed the crossing very carefully with a headstay jury-rigged from a pair of jib halyards.

The lesson learned was that, due to faulty installation or age, or perhaps for no reason at all, stainless cable is ultimately unreliable. While stays and shrouds protect the mast in the vast majority of cases, when they don't, crises of major proportions can descend upon you.

In line with my coward's rule (when dealing with the sea it's the only sort of rule to have) that ultimate crises are to be avoided, I have become convinced that, for ease of handling, for ease of reefing, and for the avoidance of the peril of dismasting, the best way to go for old sailors is with an unstayed mast.

With a stayed mast, when the stays go, the mast comes

down, whereas an unstayed mast is designed to stay up without any assistance.

Some other stay-related matters to think about:

Absent stays and shrouds and spreaders, when the time comes to climb your mast, you can just slide on up sans impalement.

All boats don't rock and sway in the same rhythm. When rafted to another vessel, should you heel to port as your neighbor heels to starboard, the chance of an interlock between spreaders and stays can cost you your mast and the eternal enmity of your neighbor.

We were required to replace a mast in Djibouti using the cranky boom of an ancient freighter. The spider web of tangling and swinging cable was daunting. An unstayed mast would have slid right in.

Or think about ice cream. As the gods would have it, a U.S. Navy destroyer rose on the horizon and came to ask us what in the world we were doing there. Satisfied with our answer, they asked if they could be of any help. "Ice cream," the lady pleaded, and in a moment a large steel ball under which was appended a gallon of vanilla ice cream descended and immediately became entangled in our port shrouds. The entanglement could have been permanent, and the mast might well have been yanked out like an unwanted weed. Luckily the same gods who responded to the lady's prayer allowed a miracle of unknotting, and we and the ice cream were saved.

I'll grant that these events don't happen every day. But happen they do.

At the risk of outraging gobs of sailors who have their own ideas about boats and sail plans, a vessel that makes enormous good sense is a Freedom 40, with a cat ketch sail plan. Because its two masts are unstayed and because two masts mean less canvas for old muscles to control, this gets my vote as possibly the best boat for the older sailor.

The next time you fly, peer out the window at the wing that's supporting your multiton aircraft as it leaps and bucks to ever-present turbulence.

Do you see any stays?

Anti-Through-Hulls

We were coming down the Red Sea, admittedly no place to ever be, when the wind shifted 180 degrees, as it always does in the middle of that crazy piece of water. I was summoned out of a deep sleep by the unaccustomed quiet and smoothness of my diesel engine. It just sounded wonderful, and I wanted to see why. Up came the floorboard, and I found myself peering at myself reflected from an almost perfect mirror composed of oil-coated bilgewater. The water level was just below the air intake when I managed to shut down the engine.

On most sailboats at a moment like this, pandemonium sets in, with everyone rushing everywhere to check on the many through-hulls that most boats have. Through-hull valves are designed to stop ingress of water in an emergency. They are another of those "safety" devices that have unsafe elements built in. In the dark, wet, scary, and heaving moment of an emergency, the problem is to find the damn things and have the strength (remember your old back) to get at these most inconveniently placed devices.

In seeking the best design for *Unlikely*, I looked backward more than forward, and I found, in an old design book, something old salts called a waterbox (see page 62).

All I had to do in my emergency was to reach down into the water, find the big yellow lever at the box, and shut it off. In a moment the rising water started to ebb. The vast majority of saltwater ingress comes from failed hoses, connectors, and pipes running from through-hull to use point. My one valve manifold shut off all incoming saltwater, giving me elderly leisure to slowly seek out the failure.

This oldfangled idea is blindingly logical and has been ignored for many years. Not only does it function in a desperate emergency, but it's also an infinitely cheaper system to build, and it reduces the many below-the-waterline holes in the hull to one. All those holes always worried me.

Anti-Unsnippable Safety Lines

Safety lines
Were designed
To save your precious heinie
But should you be
Consigned to the Sea
They trap you in the briney

You're a woman of considerable age. Your sailor husband and you are on a passage just a few miles up the coast, well in sight of land. The weather's wet but pleasant, and the boat's moving along at a satisfying clip. Suddenly your man, somewhat over-weight and in full foul-weather gear, goes overboard.

You're a good sailor and know what to do. You push the tiller over and stop dead into the wind. You bring all sails down, start the motor, and head back to where he can be plainly seen.

You pull up and stop with him in your lee, and the boat draws closer, pushed slowly by the wind, till he is next to the boat.

In this scenario, according to a U.S. Navy study done some years ago, there is a better than 50-50 chance that your husband will drown right alongside the boat before he can be brought aboard.

The problem is your stainless safety lines. Safety lines could not prevent him from going overboard, and now they add three feet or so to your freeboard, above which the sodden, panicky man must be lifted by your less-than-apelike muscles.

Not only are the safety lines a barrier to his being brought back onto the deck, but they're a particularly tricky barrier since almost anything—clothing, safety harness, belt, etc.—can (nay, will) catch on the lines. According to an ancient truism of the sea that says if anything bad can happen it will, you're left tugging at a heavy deadweight now inextricably trapped by your safety lines.

The boat gives a little lurch, and your tired and strained hands lose their grip. He plunges back into the sea as you fall backward into the cockpit with a bone-jarring thud.

The wind is now up a bit, the seas are building, and the afternoon light is fading. You're hurt and exhausted, and your husband drowns alongside your boat, just as the U.S. Navy predicted he would.

The very device that was designed to save a life now takes one. But the solution is simple.

Never, never install steel safety lines. They're killers . . . even the ones with "openable" alligators. Do the easy, cheap, and simple thing. Run Dacron line instead of the steel, and always carry a boat knife. In an emergency simply cut the safety lines. Then, when someone needs to be hauled out of the sea, there are no additional three feet to overcome, nothing to snag on, and the man overboard, now only some inches from the deck, can help in his own rescue.

Backup Starter

We were in the Greek islands when our starter motor died. With no mechanics available, I needed to contort my ancient frame to dismount the starter. It was then necessary to take an overnight ferry to Athens for a replacement—a very expensive trip that required a night in Athens because the seas were "too rough for the ferry."

Ever since this episode, I've carried a spare starter, but in the event of battery depletion a replacement starter would also be useless.

Quite by accident I ran across an ad for a "spring wound starter motor" (Pentham) operated by a pull cord. My first thought was that my old arms might not have the strength to pull the cord, but after testing by me and other Ancient Mariners, it proved to be easy to use and the absolutely best backup for either motor or battery failure.

Your primary engine starter should still be the conventional electrical model, but please, for a few hundred dollars, tuck this magic little device away among your spares.

Electronic Communications

There are all sorts of options to allow old grandfolk to speak, should they wish, to their progeny. Additionally, there are as many options, and more, for use in emergency situations.

Emergencies for all sailors are very serious business, but for the Ancient Mariner the need for quick response to assistance is absolutely imperative. Few of us oldsters have the stamina to carry us through a demanding confrontation with the sea or with our own health. What a young deck ape can easily survive is beyond the ability of us old apes. So look to your emergency communications. A few different types are described below.

Cell Phones
These ubiquitous devices are seamlessly capable of reaching assistance or of talking to a grandkid. They are, of course, limited in range, but since most of us are coast huggers, they're the recommended first line of protection.

Very High Frequency (VHF) Radio
VHF marine radio is also limited in range (to line-of-sight transmissions) and not officially monitored twenty-four hours a day, but there's always someone within 20 or 30 miles who will have his receiver on. VHF requires no expertise, and the equipment is within the financial reach of all. Channel 16 is the emergency channel. The VHF radio spectrum is 156 to 163 megahertz.

SSB Radio
Single-sideband (SSB) marine radio is for long-range communications and is always monitored by an operator. Although it's easy to use, the equipment isn't cheap, and individual calls are expensive. However, if you're a thousand miles at sea and a bit decrepit, it might be an option to consider. SSB marine radio operates at medium (2 to 3 MHz) or high (4 MHz, 6 MHz,

8 to 9 MHz, 12 MHz, 16 MHz, 18 MHz, 22 MHz, and 25 MHz) frequency bands, within which 2,182 kilohertz is the principal international distress frequency and is continuously monitored by the coast guard. Like VHF, SSB radio is easy to use.

Amateur (Ham) Radio

To be a ham operator you need an amateur radio license and a modest familiarity with radio operation. The licenses are not difficult to obtain, and an old ham will be delighted to teach you basic operating skills. Like SSB, amateur radio is for long-range communication. Its chief advantages are that all communications are free, the range is worldwide, and there are always other amateur operators listening somewhere in the world, although it is not continuously monitored by the coast guard. Ham equipment can be pricey, but last-generation transceivers can be had for relatively little.

Amateur radio once saved my life when we were 2,000 miles at sea in the mid Pacific. Personally I wouldn't go to sea without it.

Emergency Beacons

Sometimes, when we're overcome by events, we don't have the time or the ability to get out a recognizable SOS call for help. With a 406-megahertz EPIRB, response and assistance can be as fast as the time it takes any nearby vessel to reach you. This is the ultimate defense and absolutely recommended (for more on EPIRBs, see pages 57–58).

The 406 must be maintained over the years. Maintenance includes reregistration every two years. Registration allows the coast guard, which receives the distress signal, to be reasonably certain that the information on file concerning the boat make, length, and color is up-to-date. Accurate information makes it easier for searchers to find you.

Ancient Communications

Ancient Mariners have always been desperately concerned with communications, most of which in the past had to be undertaken in the worst possible circumstances.

The ancient techniques have been overcome by the ease of radio. They are little known, especially among our younger sailors, who never knew of life at sea without instantaneous electronic communications.

When all power is out and the chips are down, sailors young and old should be familiar with traditional signaling methods. However, in all my experience at sea, the only mariners who could read signal flags or signal lights have been ancient ones.

Although it's no longer likely that you'll direly need the ability to communicate by flags or lights, the techniques are easily learned, and the equipment is essentially free.

The very first thing you need to know is Morse Code. You don't need to be a whiz at it—a couple of words a minute will do for most navigational applications. Unless you're a stubborn old ham, and there are still many, you won't be messaging back and forth in code to friends and family.

Old forms of nonelectronic communication are particularly suited to us reluctant elders who resist being dragged screaming and kicking into a twenty-first-century world that is ill-suited to our twentieth-century mind-set. The best thing about these forms of communications is that when your power is out, which it's likely to be in a real crisis, the sending and receiving of letter signals always works with elegance and clarity.

All the radio beacons that guide you unerringly into safe havens are identified by a Morse signal. It's usually related to the name of the harbor into which you're sailing, but beware, not always. Navigational lights are sometimes identified by a Morse letter pattern in flashes, but beware, not always.

The passing of information by way of flags, lights, and radio waves requires that you have at hand the really delicious *In-*

ternational Book of Signals, which is my all-time favorite dream book. Anything that can happen at sea or that must be passed to land or to another vessel can be found in this compendium of two-, three-, or four-letter codes. Each of the many sections covers a specific area—for example, the section on illness or injury has hundreds of utterly simple ways to identify the exact nature of the problem.

There are letter signals that can indicate that your engines are out, that you're carrying nuclear bombs, or that you're in dire need of butter. It allows conciseness and clarity even when the winds are up and vision is difficult. If your flags can't be seen, a flashlight will do the job, and when there's just terrible radio interference, a couple of slow Morse *dit dit dah dah*s will always get through.

There's no need for memory or learning to use *The International Book of Signals*. Whoever you're signaling will have, or should have, the identical book, and the process is as simple as reading an alphabetical index of the letter codes.

Besides, there's that extra thrill of having a skill that few others know about. Being familiar with and using *The International Book of Signals* is like belonging to an exclusive club.

Computer Hell

If you know how to do long division, the chances are that you're hopelessly out of touch with your world. Such skills are better forgotten. They clutter the mind and help separate us old folk from the real world.

Most of us have accepted the sirenic message that new stuff is for the young and that, as old dogs, we're incapable of learning new tricks. Ask yourself if this message is true, or are we seeking not to be challenged? We are faced with a choice.

Should we ancient sailors hold fast to the simple and proven methods of a hundred generations of passagemaking, or must we stick our toe into the panoptic confusion of technologies that are less than one generation old?

A deeper question for old sailors is whether new cancels out old, or is new more like a welcome and sweet felicity of icing on the already moist and edible cake of experience. Can we old dogs really *not* learn new tricks? Do the blinders of experience so narrow our vision that we partake too little of the technological feast laid out before us?

Experience *can* narrow vision. If a thing works, ancient experience logically asks, why try something new? If your life at sea has involved some decades of provable techniques that have become ingrained in your very muscles, where lies the advantage of change?

These are good and germane questions, especially when our aging bodies and minds are fighting not only our years but also the widening gulf of incongruence between what we know and what the world knows.

Hemingway once described the Paris of the 1920s as a "moveable feast." Spread out before him in Paris was a smorgasbord of new ideas and sensations. Hemingway, like other experimenting artists breaking out of their Victorian corsets, dipped into this captivating stewpot of the recently forbidden. As delighted as Hemingway was in new liberties, his own writing looked back to straightforward and understandable constructions. He held tight to techniques in which he and his readers all felt comfort, while, at the same time, drawing from the moveable feast of recency.

This is exactly what we gerontic sailors must do. Although most of this book preaches and yearns for the "old ways," we should be smart enough, as Hemingway was, to pick and choose from the groaning table of ideas those that may enlarge and enrich us.

We must seek out complexities made simple. We must reduce arcane and unknowable technologies into tools as familiar as a hammer.

Or, more to the point, as familiar as a typewriter.

Most old folk approach a computer as if it were a land mine. An act as simple as touching a button becomes fraught with unknown and terrifying consequences. There's something about the ease and infinite responsiveness of a computer that unnerves those of us who've become accustomed to the concept that tools are extensions of our hands, as is a typewriter, rather than an extension of our minds, as is a computer.

Well, my friends, get over it. While you'll never know how a computer works, don't let your ignorance of the far shores of electronics lead you to assume that you'll never know how to use a computer.

Computers are designed for idiots. They require no creative thought in their use. They have no inherent logic in how you do things. They resist creative operating solutions. Computers require only that you learn the same sort of rules that make you into a sailor.

If the wind is from there, and you want to go somewhere else, do this. As a cruising sailor, you have no need to know of the physics of vectors and lift. You only need to know how, not why, to do something as spectacular as sailing against the wind or as crucial as saving your vessel.

It's the same with computers. You can do the most marvelous, undoable things with no more knowledge of "why" than the apocryphal chimps who write *Hamlet*. Your six-year-old grandson is empty-headed about why things work, but is he ever an expert on how to tame a computer and make it sing.

Although the urge for passagemaking is basically countercultural, if we oldsters are to stay in the swim, we must become computer savvy. Computers are a doorway through which we may enter into the modern world without selling out to it. Computers are sieves through which old folk can sort out the wheat of importance in sailorly lives from the chaff in which meaning is embedded. Just because we went sailing to escape the chaff doesn't mean we must leave the intellectually edible stuff behind.

Paper may be more pleasing, but charts increasingly appear as digitalized images. Ham radio, that comforting companion of passagemakers, is fading in the brilliant simplicity of e-mail and satellite cell phones useable by anyone with an index finger. Tide tables? On the Net. New navigational obstructions? On the Net. Even the Time Tic from the deep Midwest, so central to sextant navigation, is displayed to the millisecond each time you boot up your onboard computer.

Even the language is familiar. Surfing the Net. Navigating a program. What is your vessel if not a mechanism in which a "search engine" is simply a hologram?

Computer makers add complexity of use as an excuse to render perfectly good equipment obsolete. The first law of computing for old sailors is to avoid state of the art. The newest generation of software is out of your reach financially and, anyway, adds not a whit to sailorly needs. Seek out operating systems that are two or three years old (antique in the world of computers) and that have been debugged to your benefit by millions of users.

The best hardware for a sailor is a Macintosh laptop. For a few hundred dollars Macs can be had secondhand, cast off by computer nerds ever seeking complexity and challenge, two conditions that old sailors should avoid like the Caribbean in hurricane season.

Most computer problems come from the need to cable and connect various parts of a system. On a sailboat, bedeviled by salt, cabling and connecting are where problems lie. The nice thing about a Mac is that everything can be had in one case; computer, CD reader-writer, and monitor are integral, internally connected, and thus more resistant to salt.

When you get your computer, read the manual. You'll be in Computer Hell for some months, mostly because you think you're smarter than the manual. You are, but your sort of smarts don't work . . . manuals do. Your smarts are creative, which is just what basic operating systems are designed to avoid. Manuals are . . . *manual* . . . hands on, noncreative, and mechanical. To avoid becoming impatient with your computer, *please* read the manual. Kids, on the other hand, approach the computer intuitively, but you, my old friend, are no longer a kid. Read the manual.

Seek out some kid who won't be able to vote for another six years, and a child shall lead you. Don't be embarrassed. They learned their computer smarts by not being smart. Do this, they learn, and that happens . . . and never ask why.

Two exhortations.

Although computers are minor miracles, they're also irreparable at sea. Never use any system whose operation is dependent on a computer without having a backup system that isn't computer dependent.

And read your manual.

Breaks for Bad Backs

Our spines were never meant to last as long as the rest of us. Backs were designed to notify us around the age of thirty-five that, although we still had life left, it would probably not be worth living. When we moan "why me?" while getting out of bed in the morning, we must remember that the "me" is the entire human race. Bad backs are a pandemic ailment, and the older you get the worse the symptoms—so, old friend, get used to it.

However, there's no reason to abuse a bad back to the point of immobility. Care and tough love must be lavished on that crumbling structure, especially if you're an old sailor and still wish to sail.

The best way to make a bad deal worse, backwise, is to do heavy lifting. Whether you're a deep-sea voyager or a shallow-bay daysailor, there are inevitable tasks that involve the bending and the tugging for which backs were *supposed* to be designed. Most activities aboard don't require heavy lifting. But there are some that do.

If you're over fifty and your anchor weighs more than half your age, you're tempting fate by not shipping a windlass.

If you're using chain to allow you to sleep at night, then add the weight of the chain to the weight of the anchor and picture what that will do to your back, especially if things have to be done quickly.

If you have the power, by all means use an electric windlass, but never *depend on* an electric device. The backup should have a hand-operated capability that can be operated from an *upright* standing position.

The other heavy-lifting scenario involves getting heavy things off and on the boat. These heavy things are your life raft, your dinghy, and your outboard motor. These become more important when you are alongshore . . . which is most of the time.

The easiest of the three to address is the outboard. As mentioned on pages 61–62, the chief use of an outboard is to get you a hundred yards or so back and forth from shore. There's no need for a big motor since size = weight = Oh, my aching back. Check out the old salts in your harbor. Chances are that at least most of them have tiny little put-puts that are easy on both the spine and the pocketbook.

Your dinghy is much heavier than your outboard, and its awkward size and weight when out of the water add to the probability that it can land you in the costly hands of an osteopath. Dinghies can be hauled by the use of a block and tackle, but even this involves a good deal of spinal mobility of which we have precious little to spare.

Many sailors trail their dinghies, thus avoiding lifting them on and off the boat. There are arguments against this practice that center around danger to ship and crew in a squall. A dinghy astern can be a terrible instrument of destruction when the seas are up. This threat can be dealt with by cutting the dinghy loose, but who wants to give up something so expensive?

A two-person kayak is the perfect solution to 90 percent of the uses to which a dinghy is put. It'll ferry two with ease and, with one aboard, even the lightest-weight kayak will carry 150 pounds of supplies. Launching's a cinch since weight isn't a major concern. Tie a painter to it and just slide it any which way overboard. Kayaks are small enough to find a home on deck that won't interfere with sail tending, and, no small consideration, the paddling is good for your back.

A recent and terrific development in the kayak saga is an inflatable model developed by Stearns. It weighs 29 pounds, is quickly inflated—thereby eliminating the storage problem— and is more buoyant than hard kayaks. We tested one recently on a number of superannuated relics, some of whom were as old as eighty-five, and all had no difficulty in inflating it, slipping it overboard, and entering it. And a kayak doesn't need an outboard, as they're light, supple, and as easy to move as a kid to an ice cream stand. There's also an inflatable canoe by Stearns . . . not the usual toy type but a double-skinned real vessel, which is comfortable, light, and almost impossible to tip over. That's a big plus for old folk who would rather not get wet.

The most intractable problem of heavy lifting concerns your life raft. Instructions for launching are succinct: "throw it overboard." No mention is made of the hauling required to get it to and then over the rail, especially in the egregious sea states in which it would be needed.

Life rafts are inherently heavy. Additionally, they're made ever more "attractive" to buyers by the addition of mostly unnecessary elements that do more to add weight than to save lives. For old sailors, indeed for all sailors, it's more likely that the heavier a life raft is, the less likely it can be deployed without excessive pain and suffering.

The lightest raft that we could find is a four-person Winslow model configured for offshore. Sans all accessories it comes in at a stunning 31 pounds. This is about a third of the weight of other similar rafts. All of the required accessories should be stowed in a separate waterproof bag. Even old dodderers can handle this raft (for more on life rafts see page 56).

My preference is for this lightweight version, to which you've securely tied your own waterproof accessory bag, which contains all the cruising stuff that regulations require plus luxuries of your own choice. With practically a one-hand toss you can launch your 31-pound raft over the rail, followed by your accessory bag. There are many dollars to be saved by creating your own emergency supplies.

Not a small consideration is that it's usually the accessories that require annual replacement. Thus, if these delicate objects (flares, signals, food, battery-operated stuff) are stored outside the raft, you can safely delay the expensive and complicated raft-repacking agony from one year to three years.

The argument for a lightweight raft cannot be easily gainsaid. For young or old, anything heavier than a breadbasket is dangerous in rough seas. In a situation where abandoning your vessel is the only recourse, the prospect of muscling a hundredweight of mass across a bucking deck is daunting and fraught with peril. A superlightweight life raft may be the only kind that won't kill you or cripple you before you get it into the water.

For old sailors with old backs there are no options.

Meet Marv Creamer, a nonsailor until, in elder age, he took to the sea with nothing but eyes and brain. A few years ago,

Marv Creamer, a high school geography teacher with more guts than good sense and burdened by a Panglossian soul, set sail from the East Coast of the United States on an improbable passage.

Creamer, with little experience of the sea, sailed with no radio, no GPS, no log, no SatNav, no sextant, no compass, and no watch. His goal was to circumnavigate the world with nothing but his mind and eyes. He completed this barest-bones world circumnavigation safely and elegantly in seventeen months. —Reese

No One to Speak for the Stars

Since Carl Sagan departed there are only a few old sailors left to speak for his "billions and billions" of stars. Sagan's gone, but his stars are still out there, as they have been since a lost sailor ten millennia ago lifted his eyes for guidance. But the young are paying less attention. Those of us ancient enough to glory in the heft of a brass sextant, and the power it devolves on sailors, are fewer each year. Seafarers today roam the seas and always know *exactly* where they are. How dull.

Since 1960, an insignificant speck of time as the stars go, fewer sailors raise their eyes to the heavens for guidance across the empty oceans. We've replaced Sagan's glorious mystery of parsecs-distant stars with those clickety-clack little stellar imitations ... satellites. We manufacture our stars these days ... a process that at once increases our control of our lives while diminishing our ability to glory in the unknowable mysteries of the universe. We've replaced distant stars with close-by satellites, thereby reducing our vision from unknowable parsecs to a mere few hundred miles. In my book, a bad trade.

Once upon a time when crossing a big ocean, there were the very serious problems of knowing where you were, what direction you were heading, and how fast, or slow, you were getting there.

The "where you were" was dealt with by a sextant and the simple measurement of latitude by meridian transit. On a bobbing and leaping sailboat this was rarely accurate, but in the context of 3,000 miles of ocean, it was sufficient.

The "direction you were heading" became the job of your trusty compass, which never lied but also, because of the myriad discontinuities of our Earth's magnetism, never told the exact truth. The lies it told were sufficiently true to guide us across the enormous oceans.

The "how fast you were getting there" was, in olden times, determined by the eye of a salty sailor who could invariably tell speed within a knot. But in roiled-up seas these guesses might be far from accurate.

Then came the electronic revolution, and much of the thrill of sailing was displaced by the dulling accuracy of precise instrumentation. Sailing the great oceans has become less fun, less personal, and profoundly less of a deep relationship between man and nature.

To recapture the thrills of our youth and the epiphanies of our early years of ocean passaging, it is necessary to jettison the baggage of precision that denies us the oceans we sail across.

Some have already done that. The chief among them was Marv Creamer, who we met on page 83 and who circumnavigated in seventeen months sans water or wind instruments, sans GPS, sans compass, sans sextant, and even sans a timepiece. If schoolteacher Marv can manage so elegantly around the world, wouldn't most of us manage at least a nonelectronic transatlantic voyage?

I deal in this section with only the determination of speed through the water sans any man-made device. All that's required is 100 feet of line and your beating heart. It's the most elegant solution that can be imagined.

Since everything in a sailboat is imprecise anyway, let's assume that your heart beats 60 times a minute. Actually it's a little faster, although not nearly enough to affect a long-term knowledge of when you'll get to where you're going.

Attach a small drogue (or funnel or almost anything) to one end of the 100-foot line and tie a knot at the other end. Let the line pay out and count your heartbeats until you feel the knotted end. Counting 60 heartbeats means you're doing 1 knot, 30 beats means 2 knots, 20 beats means 3 knots, 15 beats means 4 knots, and 12 beats means 5 knots. Thus, sans any device, you not only know your speed through the water but also have been reminded from whence the appellation *knot* was derived, plus you've beat the bejesus out of technology.

For those of you for whom precision is king and who know that hearts, like compasses and sextants, have minds of their own and generally run at 70 beats per minute, well, just slap on an extra 5 percent.

It won't make a damn bit of difference anyway.

The first time I went to sea, I bought a Davis plastic sextant (the only one that I could afford) and set out from Morehead City, North Carolina, toward the Azores. With the Davis in one hand and Mary Blewitt's crystalline little book, *Celestial Navigation for Yachtsmen,* in the other, I committed myself and my crew to the guidance of the immutable stars. My boat, *Unlikely V,* was a 32-foot Westsail, as good a vessel as a tyro sailor could hope for, my experience was more bravado than fact, and my crew was even dumber than I, if that could be possible.

I lost my ocean virginity on that passage, in high exaltation. Celestial sights were taken daily, and I learned the hard way that an accurate sight from the deck of a leaping, swooping sailboat is more a matter of art than of science ... a trade-off I would make anytime.

My readings of sun and stars were erratic but, on the average, reassuring. Even when, at the end of the passage, I found myself 40 miles to starboard of the port of Horta, it was a small matter after a glorious passage across 3,000 miles of ocean. My achievement wasn't that I'd missed by 40 miles, but that, with the aid of the stars and a little art, I'd made it at all.

Old and Luddite as I am, I rue the passing of the stars. It's sad and feckless to gaze up at a satellite and wonder what magical mysteries it conceals. A satellite conceals nothing ... indeed, that's the basis of its usefulness. The stars conceal almost everything about themselves except the one thing important to every sailor ... where he is.

Wonder and mystery are passing from us. This generation of sailors has pulled back from the whirling spheres of Carl's heavens and is settling for the smallest sphere imaginable. Where, in the past, navigators were encouraged, with art and patience, to reach out into unimaginable mysteries to determine our place on Earth, we now push a little button and all is revealed ... except the really important stuff.

Sailor, old friend, take very good care of your old sextant. Polish it, clean it, and, by all means, practice on it. Who knows what the future of satellites may be?

However, we all know what the future of the stars is.

Reductio NON Absurdum
(or Less Is More)

STUFF NOT NEEDED
- Hot water
- On-demand freshwater
- Refrigeration
- Air-conditioning
- Watermaker
- 110-volt electrical power
- A lot of instruments

NEVER ENOUGH OF STUFF
- Extra sails
- Bilge pumps
- Canned tuna

NOT NECESSARY BUT NICE STUFF
- Solar power
- Wind power
- Self-steering wind vane
- Black-and-white radar

DE RIGUEUR STUFF
- Life raft

MOSTLY NECESSARY BUT A PAIN IN THE ASS
- The diesel power you need:
  one foot = one horsepower

This section is meant for those remarkable folk who are cut from the same cloth as Marv Creamer, who circumnavigated without electronics, compass, sextant, or watch, and the Pardeys, who simply threw their diesel overboard and sailed the wide waters of the world in a true sailboat. For the rest of us, who may not be able to handle Amish stringency in equipping their vessels, we may pick and choose from the advice herein offered.

Ideally, an old sailor's boat should provide the maximum of opportunity for enjoyment at the least cost in effort and dollars, both of which become scarce as we grow older. Contrary to expensive ads for labor-saving stuff, the best solution for us old guys is achieved by deep-sixing (or better yet, not installing) all the high-tech, high-price gizmos that, when you come down to it, are little more than toys for people with more money than good sense and an excess of time and energy for maintenance.

Old guys, on the whole, live on strictured retirement funds, and as age creeps in, the energy required to endlessly repair and maintain complicated equipment, which is claimed to make the sailorly life easier but which only tends to make the time at sea shorter, creeps out apace.

At the most provident minimum all we really need to expand sailing time (and lifetime) is a long stick, a rag to hang on it, and something hollow to keep the water out. Anything else requires attention and dollars, and although I don't propose absolute minimalism, which is really reductio ad absurdum, we should look very closely at stuff that we add to this minimum.

Stuff Not Needed

Hot Water

Why bother? Old sailors know that showering is wasteful of precious water and, if it's hot, of power. The truth is that after a few days all the crew smells the same, as your nose is not abused by strange odors.

On-Demand Freshwater Supply

Do you really need a complicated and delicate pumping and sensing system to deliver freshwater from your tanks? I don't think so, since it can be just as easily accomplished by a simple foot pump requiring only a light tap of even an arthritic foot.

Refrigeration

If you must have refrigeration to provide cooling of alcohol and colas that you, at your age, should have long since forsworn, stay home.

Foods that must be refrigerated have no place on a sailboat. For the sort of sailing that you'll be doing—say, up to a week out of port—stick to foods that don't rot. Unrefrigerated eggs last a month, cabbages last longer, and cans last forever. Fresh meat smells up the boat and leads to tummy problems. Fresh fish should be caught and eaten the same day. The only problem I ever had was with warmish UHT (ultrahigh temperature) milk (which lasts forever), as I was raised on ice-cold milk. But I got used to it, and so will you. Water should be drunk at room temperature, and anyway, it will come cooled out of your tanks.

Banning refrigeration eliminates one more mechanical system that, like others, the engineers have been unable to tame.

Air-Conditioning

Air-conditioning is expensive, is noisy, and denies you the wonderful distressing dulcets of the sea. The chief advantage of a $3,000 air-conditioning system is that it discourages mosquitoes. But so will $10 worth of screening.

Watermaker

Sailboats easily carry up to 100 gallons of freshwater. At two quarts a day for two people, it would take a month to empty your tanks, not even considering the rain supplied by the Great Water Maker in the Sky. On a scale of ten, a watermaker rates an absolute zero.

110-Volt Power

Having 110 volts of power creates yet one more system of hot wiring that's a threat to your vessel. And unless you're foolish enough to invest in a microwave oven, your 12-volt system will power everything you should need, even TV.

Instrumentation

A chip of wood and a watch (on page 85 I describe estimating speed sans watch) provide your speed, and within a couple of months you'll be able to guess at your speed within half a knot. If you must know wind speed, a few dollars for a handheld mechanical device (that needs no maintenance) will suffice. A 10-cent piece of ribbon tied to your stays demonstrates perfectly adequately your angle on the wind.

Stuff of Which You Can Never Have Enough

Extra Sails

No matter how long a passage, across an ocean or across a bay, sails are your most fragile, quintessential resource for coming to terms with the sea. Torn sails, at best, can ruin your day or, at worst, can sink you.

Bilge Pumps

It's handy to have a bilge pump powered by your engine, two 12-volt automatic pumps, and any number of installed manual pumps. A bundle of navy-type lift pumps is nice to have. A small rotary pump attached to a 12-volt drill is nice but won't move a lot of water.

Canned Tuna

Canned tuna is the magic food of the sea. It lasts forever, needs no cooking or heating, and is capable, like love and art, of infinite variety. You can never have too much canned tuna.

Not Necessary But Nice

Power from the Sky

Solar panels and a wind generator are gifts of nature. Windmills are obtrusive and require some maintenance but deliver a fair amount of power. Solar panels are silent and unobtrusive, require no maintenance, and will trickle enough power into your batteries to keep them up to snuff. Incidentally, don't install more batteries than you absolutely need. Batteries require endless care of water levels, and too many batteries will break your old back, as they must be installed deep in the bowels of your boat because of their weight.

Escape from the Tiller

All of us have lived through those endless hours of enslavement to the tiller, hours of boredom in which only the slightest human care is needed to keep on course. It's better to have some clever device that will listen to the wind and keep you on course. Wind vane steering, something akin to the great and dependable Aeres steerers, will keep you on course in even the lightest of zephyrs and require no drain on your precious store of electrical power. There is, admittedly, a deep-seated pleasure in being at the wheel, but not being required to be there is nearly as good.

See No Evil

The only piece of complicated, irreparable technology without which I'm uncomfortable is radar. However, a ten-year-old, secondhand, black-and-white instrument will get you through a tough spot as well as one that'll blow your budget to hell. In a confrontation with Ethiopian gunboats one dark night, only radar saved my vessel. On another windy and moonless night in the Aegean, radar was the only means to pick out an island entrance barely the width of my beam. The tales are endless, as are the prices; go cheap and stay away from color.

De Rigueur

The Last Resort

An imprudent sailor started out from Los Angeles to sail the few miles to Catalina Island. Two months later, sans mast, he was picked up hundreds of miles west in the deep Pacific, heading inexorably toward Tahiti. He didn't have a life raft, and if his problem had been a hole in the hull instead of a lost mast, he would've been feeding the fishes. Although life rafts are expensive and require maintenance, *never* go to sea without one. Buy the cheapest you can find; the most expensive models do little more than drain your pocket. Incidentally, step into a life raft only when it's floating higher than your sinking deck. It's a testament to modern hulls that they stay afloat in extricable conditions for months after they've been abandoned. Don't panic; stay with your boat, which gives our creaky frames infinitely more comfort and safety than any raft ever designed.

Mostly Necessary but a Pain in the Ass

Horses

Except for the excellent few who don't need a motor, we all need propulsion. That's complicated enough, but too many of us overpower our vessels with huge, heavy, and demanding engines. A sailboat will only go so fast, so added horsepower is a useless burden.

A good rule of thumb is that one horsepower is all that's required to satisfactorily push along one foot of overall length. You can have a little more or a bit less power, but aim for the one-to-one rule.

Health and Welfare

Belief

It is silly to believe
That sighting dolphins
Assures a safe passage
I know better.

It is silly to believe
That St. Elmo and Ganesh
Smooth the sailor's way.
I know better.

But do I?
Since what I know
Is substantially less
Than what I believe.

I met Ed by accident at his very first Annapolis Boat Show. He'd known my father in his youth, and that made us fast friends. I liked Ed for his wide smile as much as for his energy and enthusiasm. At the show he sought my advice on a boat he'd chosen, and when I told him it was the worst possible choice he could make . . . he bought the boat.

What Ed fails to reveal in his comments is that he's decided to live forever. To accomplish this not inconsiderable feat, Ed puts himself through a health regimen that most of us would prefer not to live through, no matter how many more years are granted.

On one Atlantic crossing Ed was out on the foredeck every morning doing stretches on one leg while I could barely survive the leaping of the vessel while I was lying on deck and holding on with both hands. During this passage he maintained a rigorous vegetarian diet, dosed himself enthusiastically with vitamins, and, strangest of all, insisted that the entire crew do aromatherapy.

This involved the smelling of an array of vials that would indicate the alimentary intake of which we were in need. While this may sound a bit goofy, I must confess that I never had a healthier crossing. —Reese

Ed Kane on Lifestyle Changes

Lifestyle changes can take many forms, exciting as hell or dreary, dull, you name it. After spending thirty years in business, I was itching for excitement, but more than that, I desperately needed a different dimension.

The thought of sailing is totally intoxicating. Shopping for a boat that will transform your dull, dreary lifestyle is so absolutely soul filling that you don't even have to buy one. The days of perusing sailing magazines and going to boat shows brought joy like no other. I knew every manufacturer, every model, every type and style. I thought my choice of a 53-foot ketch was nothing short of brilliant until I sought out my old friend Reese Palley. He proceeded to shoot holes in my choice. There was no way it would sail . . . and it would probably kill me.

But I was determined. I bought it in 1988, sailed the Mediterranean—France, Italy, Greece, Spain—and then sailed the Atlantic. I doubt that I'll ever repeat my adventure at the helm, but I wouldn't trade that time for a skillion. It's given me that extra dimension that my life had lacked.

I reminisce how I used to pull into a new harbor and execute a flawless docking procedure. I looked like I'd been at this all my life. The dockhands would rush up to help with the line and address me as "Captain." Let me tell you, it doesn't get much better than that.

('Twas easy; I had bow thrusters, totally below waterline and out of sight.)

—Ed Kane, 2002

Limits and Reserves

One benefit of sailing is that it slows down aging by forcing upon us constant movement and isotonic exercise. Another is that it demonstrates to the sailor how to adjust to the bothersome and vexatious matters that come with aging.

If we would but listen to our sailing vessels and recognize how they abide by their needs and limits, we could learn the great lesson of aging. It's a simple lesson: your body, like your vessel, is designed to function best below its extreme design limits.

The most abusive tactic of which tyro sailors are guilty is overpowering their vessel. A sailboat's mast, hull, and gear are designed to accept enormous strains for very short periods of time and reasonable strains for a very, very long time. In crisis moments, when quick and extreme motions are needed for survival, your well-found boat will rise to the occasion. If the strain is continued for long periods of time, as in racing, weaknesses will be winnowed out, and failure will occur.

Suppose, in the interest of testing the limits of the human body, we were to posit the same kind of regimen on humans for experimental purposes. The Nazi regime did just that. In order to see how much cold a human can take it submerged subjects in ice water until their limit was reached. In this case the limit was death.

Reaching limits is not for old sailors. We're not the deck apes we used to be. Although we might be able to urge that extra iota of speed from our vessel, we probably lack the stamina required to deal with a snapped mast or a jib caught under the bow. The lesson for Ancient Mariners is clear: don't test limits of either your old vessel or your old self.

Old sailors, should they desire to sail into the last thirty years of their lives, must measure and delimit the amount of effort and energy expended. We must be acutely aware of how long a period we can afford to remain profligate of our increasingly limited reserves. There's always the temptation that appearing to be young and hale is the same thing as being young and hale. It's not, but ego drives all of us to extremes. Too may of us feel that aging is somehow shameful and must be hidden behind the veil of foolish expenditure of effort.

Slow down and take a lesson from your beloved boat, which is, possibly, a bit smarter than you are when it comes to the uses of energy. Indeed, the physics of sailing always deals with using just the exact amount of energy to get a task done. A reckless smidgeon more of effort after hull speed is reached means no more speed achieved, and a conservative smidgeon less of effort rarely affects speed at all.

Your sailing boat's displacement hull has natural limits that seriously contradict the argument that "effort in" has a relationship to "effort out." Your boat has a hull speed that can only be minutely exceeded; doing so will shorten her life and perhaps yours. Push as hard as you like, but most displacement hulls, on the average, will manage between 100 and 125 miles in a twenty-four-hour day. Double your push, hire deck apes, pile on more sail, and the chances are that if you don't break something, lines or limbs, you'll actually slow the boat down. You can walk faster than 5 knots, and if this magisterial pace doesn't suit you, find a different way of life.

Much the same is true of your old body. A young animal is capable of moments—in times of danger, for example—when it can be pushed well beyond what would be considered normal physical limits. But old sailors, especially old and experienced salts, know that their limits are quickly reached, reserves are scarce, and survival of really bad moments at sea, or even just responding to a quick squall, mostly depends on patience, cautious inactivity, and avoiding the depletion of reserves.

The best way to keep an old boat young is to discover its hull speed and then back off a knot. The best way to keep an old sailor young is exactly the same process. Discover your own physical limits and . . . back off a notch.

Move or Die

Exercise, in our culture, is something we don't do. The automobile and the ease that it gives us shorten our lives by as much time as not smoking lengthens it. The human body was designed to be used ... there's no preordained total amount of activity that, if used up, means there's nothing left. You simply *must* find an inescapable way to shake your ass. A way that you can't, in a cowardly manner, find excuses to avoid.

Elsewhere in this book I argue in detail the health advantages of a sailboat. How it helps you shed pounds, if only because you're a bit nauseous. How it keeps you trim by the lack of endless gustatory temptations. And how, for us old-timers, it lengthens life by lending meaning and relevance.

We all know of the endless muscular activity that a sailboat demands as it sways to and fro in even a kindly sea. For old bones and tendons this becomes a nonjarring stretch and release that quickly tones the body.

The highest example of fraud about exercise programs is the egregious electric belts that twitch your abdominal muscles and promise that this action is exercise. It isn't. It's delusional to call this exercise, and the only benefit derived is the profit to the seller.

"Real" exercise, which involves muscle-strengthening, or isotonic, exercises, requires purposeful activity that isn't automatic. We might sit at the wheel clenching, unclenching, or twitching with little benefit until we get up and move about the boat. Directed movement—hauling, stretching, crawling, climbing—is the essence of useful, isotonic exercises.

Isotonics hurt. More so at sea than on land, and even more so for old sailors, who, with the natural progression of age, have accumulated various skeletal aches and pains. It takes real effort to go isotonic, which is the essence of health-giving, invigorating, stretching activities.

The crazy mantra of the muscle builders and deck apes is "No pain, no gain." For us ancients, we already have the pain. There's no need to manufacture it, so we might just as well reach out, as a pure bonus, for the gain.

Did You Ever See a Fat Sailor?

Not often.

And *never* an old fat sailor.

Shouldn't we wonder why all of those nifty folk who spend their time on sailboats have loose and rangy bodies?

Fat sneaks up on you, dominates your life, alters your self-image, chases love, and drives you, in desperation, to spend sweaty hours in expensive exercise spas.

Spas are not free. It costs time and money to use the intricate, sometimes ludicrous, equipment that's designed to do what we could do ourselves if we would only get off the couch. Pulling machines, pushing machines, bending machines, stretching machines, and rowing machines are only highly chromed imitations of those healthy exertions in which sailors are involved every time they step aboard their boats.

Sailors young and old pull ropes, wind winch handles, and bend every which way, even some ways that they can't. They stretch for the sails, and when the outboard motor on the dinghy goes belly-up, which it always does, they row. All this is imitated by the chromed contraptions that, like many other things in your ancient experience, promise but don't deliver. As we graduate into the far reaches of age, we discover that the only promises that are ever truly kept are the ones we make to ourselves.

With fat gaining on our culture every year, the commercial peddlers of thin are pushing isometrics. This system of exercises is supposed to allow you to use your muscles without moving from where you're sitting, without acknowledging that sitting is the core of the fat problem.

Isotonics were invented the first time some brave soul in antiquity stepped aboard something that floated, hung up a couple of skins, and tried to make his craft go somewhere. Iso-marinetonics come free with every sailboat. It's an extra-added attraction that diminishes your waistline as it tightens flab. The thinning is generated by the endless motion of the sea imparted to your rocky little vessel. In order to survive aboard a sailboat it's necessary to clench and release every muscle of your body a thousand times a day. It's the *ne plus ultra* toning process and, if pursued beyond your middle years, can keep your old frame taut and trim in old age.

Sailing cuts down on food intake. On land we eat mostly out of boredom. On land we have too much food too easily available to us. On a sailboat boredom is a condition only vaguely recalled, so stuffing your face in front of the tube out of ennui is forsworn. Rich foods—meats and fats and cakes and breads—don't keep well in a marine environment, so should a surge of gluttony overtake you at sea, you're likely to find only healthy stuff to eat. I discovered as I progressed into my seventies that my digestive system prefers simple, familiar foodstuffs. On a sailing passage variety is perforce limited . . . and thus healthier.

Getting a meal together on a boat under way is so much work that it's not uncommon to skip eating rather than to cook. Preparing a meal at sea is hard, hard work. As we eat less because it's hard work, we work harder for the less we eat.

Even the most salty old sailors are, if not seasick, then endemically "aware" of a background roil in their digestive systems. No experienced sailor would dream of gustatory self-abuse when discomfort is already just ahead of gluttony, and a hint of nausea is our constant companion.

Fat is more and more the norm onshore today in spite of diets, exercise machines, spas, "light" foods, and fat-free foods.

Nothing seems to work. As we gain years, we gain pounds. Each pound gained slows us as we naturally slow down in the aging process. This, in turn, makes the exertion necessary to shed unneeded, unwanted, and unattractive fat that much more difficult. Fat is a self-accreting prophecy.

When we hie ourselves out to sea, we banish many of the normal processes of aging, and we also banish fat. We feel free to present to sun and moon our skinny, sea-tightened, rounded rumps. We allow the thin person inside our aging bodies to escape the burdening, burgeoning envelope of sloth. We acquire a nifty tan and the pleasure, so long avoided, to once again peer at ourselves in full-length mirrors. And, no small matter, the pleasures of sex can be outstanding.

Fat old persons arise! You have everything to lose!

The Most Dangerous Orifice: What Thou Shalt and Shalt Not Eat

The most dangerous orifice in your body is your mouth.

It's easy to get into terrible trouble not only by what we say but also by what we eat. Marilyn and I have no rules for avoiding vocal confrontations other than to advise that you keep your mouth shut. But we have strong rules concerning that other deleterious function of your mouth ... eating.

If you're planning a long cruise, perhaps even crossing an ocean, then, should you ignore the recommendations in this book, you put your old gut at risk.

We profess no scientific basis for what we offer here; however, since the nutritionists are the broken field runners of science, considering how often they reverse themselves, we feel safe in depending on the most ancient technique for determining what a sailor should eat at sea ... to wit, experience, which is the exclusive purview of age.

The curious thing, discovered after more decades at sea than we care to admit to, is that the rules outlined here for eating at sea are exactly the same rules that we should have been following, anyway, on land. At sea, where all of us, the best sailors and the worst, suffer the inner-ear disturbance and whoops of the sea, the breaking of these simple rules leads to even more egregious results than if you're on solid ground and could ease the turmoil in your gut.

The first rule for a long-distance sailor is a curious one and is contrary to what seems logical: never use a fridge at sea. If you have a fridge, you'll be using precious power for keeping foods that you shouldn't be eating anyway. The logical second rule of cruising gustation is, therefore, carry no foods that spoil.

Meat, which is alimentally egregious even on land, is the chief of the class of rotting foods to avoid. Meat spoils eventually even under refrigeration, is difficult to digest, provides too much energy for ocean passages (which, much to the contrary of common opinion, require very little), and is expensive. Add to the cost of meat the cost of preservation and the ever-present risk of food poisoning, and you've increased the cost of your cruise, which, to most retired sailors, is just another way of lessening the length of time we can afford to be at sea.

Cooked meat stays with you too long, not only in your belly but also in your nose since the smells of cooking permeate hair, boat, and clothes and require an increase in precious water use for showering.

Cooking meat is always a mess. Cleaning up after the morning bacon or the evening steak in a nasty seaway takes time and energy and, if you're dealing with searingly hot oils, can, and often does, lead to nasty burns.

Fish is also a bit too rich in protein as well as being even more subject to spoilage. Poisoning from bad fish is common on land. Who needs a belly full of finny toxins to add to big seas belaboring your inner ear already with nausea?

Cooking fish also stinks up the boat; undercooking fish (and there's no other way fish should be eaten) adds to the risk of noxious intestinal developments.

Canned fish is OK. For tuna and sardines no cooking is required, and there are no smells and little chance of spoilage. Tuna goes great with mayonnaise, which won't spoil if kept in small airtight containers, and sardines are a great treat with mustard, equally resistant to the passage of time and temperature.

The nice thing about canned fish is that, for some reason, one tends not to eat too much so that high protein ingestion is limited. However, get your canned tuna preserved in water, and get your sardines in mustard . . . watch out for the cans loaded with unnamed and questionable oils.

Cast out all white-sugar-laden treats. Candy, chocolate, and other comfort foods add not a whit to your passage and too much to your waistline. Most sailors with too many decades behind them are somewhat inefficient in absorbing sugar, so why add insult to the injuries of age?

Do not encourage sugary foods, which, like high-protein foods, will go to your belly when they have no other way to exit your body. There's a small window of satisfaction in the natural sugars of jellies, jams, and honey. Used in moderation a bit of jam for the royal slice of bread is like the sound of a boy's choir ... high, sweet, and subtly satisfying. The best of the preserves are the bitter citrus types made without added sugar. Too sweet quickly cloys. The very best we ever encountered was an Egyptian concoction made from the sour grapefruit of the Nile.

None of us are so pure and high-minded that we can long exist without some kind of treat. Those who say they can are liars. So for all of us weak and pitiable folk who need their oral "blankies," we recommend—you'll never guess—popcorn. Not the kind that emits the sickening stench of rancid butter in our movie lobbies ... all that's good for is to keep the kids quiet. One can soon develop a taste and a passion for popcorn sans butter. Contaminants only mask the simple-hearted, light, and artless flavor of unadorned popcorn of which you may, without guilt and with little abuse to your gut, eat to satiety. Hot popcorn is incredible on a cold night on watch, as the flavor and the promise of warmth and comfort float up the companionway hatch just ahead of the arrival of the steaming bowl. On one passage up the Red Sea, we had a popcorn fest with our Kiwi crew. The aroma of a popcorn treat being concocted in the galley (see recipes beginning on page 107) enriched a long passage without enriching our love handles.

Who really needs butter? What does a slab of fattening, oily, and smelly white grease add to your passage? Even margarine, while less damaging to your heart than butter, has little that's socially or sailorly beneficial. Same for ice cream, cream cheese, and cream in your coffee.

We must admit one personal lactic exception. A good hard cheese that can roll about unrefrigerated in the bottom of a locker for months is hard to resist. Admittedly, cheese is formidable to digestion, attacks your arteries, and pumps up the tire about your waist, but as a rare and special treat, with half a glass of red wine and some Kalamata olives, there's little to beat it at sea or on land. Incidentally, olives keep just about forever.

Eggs are interesting. They keep *without refrigeration* for as long as it takes to cross an ocean. There are lots of ways to prepare eggs, and in moderation, they can be forgiven their protein and their cholesterol.

Green veggies spoil quickly. There's one noble and notable exception: cabbage. Cabbage is good for you, lasts a long time, supplies fiber, isn't fattening, makes a dynamite soup and satisfying slaws, and is the mate for corned-beef-less cabbage. Americans look down their narrow Western European noses at cabbage, while Eastern Europeans, for eons, have been secretly concocting wondrous dishes such as borscht, stuffed sweet-and-sour cabbage rolls, and pickled whole cabbages. Peasant food. But in the final analysis it's really peasant foods that go best on a boat.

For example, there's pasta. A truly peasant food. There's nothing, absolutely nothing, that you can do to pasta that will exaggerate how you experience the motion of your vessel. Pasta sinks solidly down into the belly, produces no odoriferous belchy emanations, and is, digestively speaking, most obliging. In all our experience we've found that plain pasta is the best antidote for the Sickness of the Sea.

Cooking pasta requires no hot oils, and should your fresh water be running low, pasta allows itself to be tastefully cooked in sea water. Pasta, like love, is capable of intriguing variation. As in lovemaking, anything that you can think of adding to pasta will only improve it.

One likes to think that pasta was invented not by Italians but by some ancient sailor who got sick and tired of rotting foods. And pasta comes with that special talent that's desired above all others by a sailor . . . it won't spoil, stale, or rot. We bought pasta in Romania in 1989. We bought a lot of it since it was very cheap in those days when the dollar was the sailor's friend. We stashed pasta in every conceivable crevice. We crammed it under bunks and into the PVC tubes we roll our charts in. It's beyond belief how much pasta can be inserted into the fissures, chinks, and crevices, otherwise wasted space, of any sailboat. We ate pasta with abandon because of the knowledge of endless supply, and we continued to do so for the next five years, the same pasta that we bought in the grocery store of Constanza when we pulled into that Romanian port. Pasta: the sailor's friend.

Bread is good, but it stales quickly, so you have to learn to bake aboard. To bake, you must carry flour; the problem with flour is that no matter how pure the stuff looks when you buy it, wee insects appear nearly spontaneously and disturb the more fastidious among us. The less fastidious have learned that the bit of protein represented by the mites does no harm ... except aesthetically.

For those who are wary of the wigglies there's a perfect means of preservation of flour as well as other dried stuff such as beans and cereals. Before sailing, place a small piece of dry ice in the bottom of a quart plastic jug. Pour in the flour or whatever and leave the cap loose for a couple of hours. In that time the dry ice melts and permeates the jar with carbon dioxide, inimical to all wiggly life but harmless to you. Tighten down the cap, and in ten years no creatures will appear.

As a pretty fair substitute for bread, try to find the five-gallon tins of hard plain crackers that, with a shot of grog, spread by the English Empire around the world. They can get a bit moldy, so break down the big containers into little airtight ones. If you can't find the English variety, there's a cracker made in Cuba that will do just as well. They usually come packed in small sealed cellophane packages, so they require no repacking and can be tucked away into almost any unlikely empty nook on the boat.

Now for some specifics.

Recipes

Here are a few of the utterly simple and blindingly sensible recipes that have sustained us for our twenty years at sea and in later years have proven kindly to diminished digestive tracts. By following these recipes while at sea, we've become svelte and slim. Alas, for those odd months we were forced to spend ashore, some of the svelteness changed back to fat. The only cure was to go back to sea. Not at all a bad medicine.

Fish Cakes
Mash together canned tuna or salmon with chopped fresh or dried onions, and add egg (to moisten). Roll and coat with bread crumbs and then panfry in a little—very little—olive oil.

Cabbage and Potato Soup
Boil together in large pot of water cut-up cabbage, onions, and potatoes with chicken bouillon cubes, salt, and pepper.

Pasta Putanesca
Serve boiled pasta with a drizzle of olive oil, any canned veggies, and a sprinkle of processed (canned) Parmesan cheese.

Kugel
Moisten leftover, unadorned pasta with beaten egg and mixed with honey, cinnamon, and raisins; bake.

Bread Pudding
Moisten leftover stale bread and crackers with egg and a small can of evaporated milk or UHT milk; mix in honey, cinnamon, and raisins or canned fruit and then bake. If no oven, panfry as a pancake.

Popcorn
Popcorn + olive oil + garlic powder + salt
Popcorn + a wisp of honey
Popcorn + olive oil + cayenne pepper
Popcorn + cinnamon + canola oil
Popcorn + olive oil + grated cheese
Popcorn with salt
Plain popcorn

KISYSOS—Keep It Simple, You Silly Old Salt
The best advice for all sailors is to keep meals simple and fla-
vorful. Don't go too heavy on the spices, as they'll repeat maybe
even days later. As the sea change overtakes you, your senses
will sharpen and amplify. Aromas heretofore slighted by your
smell-abused nose on land will waft up the companionway,
teasing your taste buds and burying your queasiness. Even basic meals will be gourmet, and the pounds shed by sensible eating will add years to your sailing life.

As we age, pounds added become increasingly difficult to
shed. The best by far dietary advice is to limit your intake of
food. Changing what you eat is considerably less important to
your body than how much you eat. It's quantity in the end, and
I do mean in the end, that leads to obesity, and while it's rare
to find a fat sailor, it's better not to take any chances.

Keep your mouth, that most dangerous orifice, shut when
at all possible.

Limber Up

The Oxford English Dictionary gives a number of definitions for the word *limber*. One definition of *limber holes* still carries the meaning of passing unwanted water to a sump. The earliest record of the word is in 1480, and by 1565 the word had been converted into the modern meaning of pliant, supple, and lithe.

Whatever its derivation, it describes a bodily condition that should be of great interest to Ancient Mariners. The *un*-limbering of your body will put an early end to your sailing life. Remaining limber is a product of a number of factors, including continuing physical activity, strict control of accumulation of fat, and, of course, stretching.

Old tendons shorten up and must be increasingly and consciously stretched as you age. Stretching is one of those blessed activities that not only are good for you but *feel* good, too. It also can be done anywhere, at any time, under any condition.

Sailors have an advantage in this over the land (and muscle) bound. Sailors always stretch while underway and even in port, considering the contortions necessary to navigate the close confines of a sailboat even when it's at rest.

Stretching shouldn't be left to accidental movements. Stretching must include and consider all of the muscles and tendons. This can be accomplished only by a careful and scientific approach. Try some stretches . . . your old body will be grateful.

For a good book on the topic see *Stretching* by Bob Anderson (illustrated by Jean Anderson, 20th anniversary, revised edition, Shelter Publications, 2000). Pay particular attention to the chapter titled "Stretches for Those Over 60!" (pages 120–21). Anderson includes stretches for the neck, shoulders, arms, back, chest, groin, hips, legs, and feet.

It's certainly not necessary to do all of these stretches each time. Also, some may not be possible or comfortable in the restricted area of your vessel. Do as many as you can. If time is a constraint, vary the stretches you do in each session.

Just remember to S-T-R-E-T-C-H.

Abs of Steel

Lower back pains are the Lord's reminder that he's not perfect. We probably were never intended to walk upright, and we pay for this extension of our horizon by abuse of our lower sacra. Sacra are held in place by the bands of muscles, *abs* in common parlance, that encircle them. When your abs go, sacra start grinding against each other, and what starts out as a minor annoyance can, in advanced age, incapacitate you.

There are some really nifty exercises that are designed to produce abs of steel. The problem is that these are designed for use on a solid surface that is not, as on your sailing vessel, jumping about like a Mexican low rider. Additionally, there's little if any flat surface available, so here are three exercises that are designed to be used in your bunk.

Before you get out of bed, while you still have a relatively stable surface, do these abs of steel exercises.

1. Stretch. As you lie on your back, pull first one leg and then the other tightly up against your chest. This doesn't do much for your abs, but it provides the necessary stretch for the next steps.

2. Crunch. While still in your bunk and without help from your arms, lie as flat on your back as you can, keep your knees together, and pull them tightly against your chest using only your ab muscles. Do this fifty times each morning. This is tough. It seems impossible at first, but within a week or two things will ease, and in a month or two it will become an easy habit.

3. Crunch. With your feet flat on your bunk, pull your head and shoulders off the bed using only your abs. This is a relatively easy exercise, so you should have no trouble doing it one hundred times.

For the Ancient Mariner who wakes up a bit creaky, these stretches will get the blood running. As a bonus, in the short run they'll dekink your morning back. In the long run you'll glance at yourself in the mirror one day and be rewarded with the dips and hollows of abs of steel.

A Whack on My Old Back

A few years ago I received a belated sixtieth birthday present from my sailboat. The gift was a whack on the back, which I'm sure most of you old salts have also experienced at some time, whether from a boat or some other source. The whack troubled me for a few months and then subsided until Hurricane Georges hit Key West. During those terrible hours and the even more terrible aftermath, I far exceeded the physical limits of my decades-old spine.

Since then, with symptoms increasing, I was terrified that I might never be able to sail my beloved (but sneaky) *Unlikely* again.

To effect a cure, I set out to survey the entire spinal medical experience. In the beginning most docs said, "Live with it; at your age what do you expect?" Images of ocean passages receded as I descended ever lower on the professional scale, listening to whiffy lectures recommending acupuncture, yoga, aromatherapy, and other arcane paramedical nostra. But I was desperate to get to sea again, so feeling not a little foolish, I tried them all. Needless to say, my ancient back shrugged off the prickings and the proddings and the smellings and continued to hurt. Matters were looking bleak, indeed.

Finally, I ended up in the hands of a physical therapist. She gave me a series of stretching exercises that she guaranteed would *not* cure my condition but that might limber me up a bit. I dutifully stretched and twisted and otherwise contorted my old frame into untenable positions. Surprisingly, the pretzeling seemed to help.

In the midst of all of this activity, I was visited by a troubling wisp of recall. In a flash of déjà vu, it came to me that I'd done all this stuff before. The very contortioning that I was consciously practicing on dry land in order to get back to sea was what I'd always done unconsciously by simply being at sea on my boat in even the mildest of seaways.

Banish your fears that you'll never be able to leap about

again. Don't worry that you won't be able to sail, as the very act of sailing has in it the seeds of limberness. My boat, it turned out, was a much better cure than all the rest of the spinal folderol.

The solution is to get to sea as quickly as possible and give yourself up to the endless therapy of your vessel as she pulls, twists, and bends every muscle, every ligament, every joint of your body. What you had always considered discomfort you can now admire as cure. Your boat offers more encompassing, lasting therapy than you could ever get on land.

Let's consider some of the exercises that were recommended to me by the therapist. Start with a limbering of the hips. The first joints that lock up with an initial twinge of back pain are your hips. You can no longer rumba, and the tango is unthinkable. Now recall what happens to you as you stand at the wheel of your sailboat. The yawing and pitching and listing are transported up your exercising legs and unlock your hips in a dance that resembles nothing more than a maritime twist. Thus, the first thing you can do to strengthen your back is to steer your boat . . . from a standing, never a sitting, position.

The next procedure my therapist laid on me was to strengthen my abs. Bend, crouch, flex those abs, she said, which is simply what happens on a moving sailboat all the time, anywhere on the boat you happen to be. Hatches must be bent over, passageways ducked through, and supplies rummaged out of the deepest, most unreachable storage recesses. Keep this up, and a washboard gut of steel can't be far away.

Then the therapist had me lie down and twist my legs first to one side and then to the other. Big deal . . . that's all I ever do in my bunk as my legs almost automatically brace against first a swing to starboard and then to port. My spread legs are the only things keeping me flat on my back.

Reaching and straightening the spine was another exercise. So what's so new about that . . . ask any sailor about reaching up to haul a mainsail or stretching out to haul in an anchor.

As imaginative as my therapist was, she never even came close to the stretchy opportunities that a sailboat provides. How do you duplicate lying on deck at the bow, bracing with both legs against the pitch of the sea and at the same time bringing in a recalcitrant foresail? Can't do it on land.

Going to the john on land is a far cry from going to the head on a boat. With your vessel trying mightily to hurl you embarrassingly about, you stretch arms and legs to walls and ceilings just to keep yourself firmly potted. The thought of being dethroned in mid-evacuation is enough to lend protean strength to your back. And you have to do it several times a day!

But the ultimate lubricant, the absolutely final stretches possible for the human frame, will take place in the engine compartment into which you must periodically thread yourself. Picture this: the sea is running heavily enough to ferret out a weakness in your engine. When, not if, it stops, you must then descend into the impossibly small and discontiguous spaces that surround a very hot engine. In an attempt, usually feckless, to avoid thermal epidermal abuse and at the same time to reach that stubborn nut with your wrench, you (a stubborn nut of a different sort) contort to the conterminous limit of muscles, ligaments, tissues, and patience. By simply approaching your engine, confined as it is in an ungenerous area, let alone actually working on it upside down as you usually must, you've accomplished more physical therapy than has ever been dreamed of in the therapist's philosophy.

Some may complain that the demands of a moving sailboat might place too much strain on an already iffy back. To these naysayers I offer the advice of my therapist, who said, when she gave me instructions for her procedures, "Do it until it hurts, then stop . . . " ("stupid" was elided).

It's almost the same on a sailboat. Do your normal sailorly duties, slowly and thoughtfully, and do them until it hurts; do them just a little more . . . then stop.

But never, never, never stop sailing.

Toes and Feet

All of us have experienced a sensation that our feet are colder than the rest of us. Our fingers and toes get their blood supply through smaller and smaller vessels. These microarteries and veins are the first to lose the ability to supply blood as our bodies age. When we old folk go in for our regular checkups, the first thing that a good doc will do is to feel for a pulse just below your ankle bone and to feel, with his hands, the temperature of your feet.

All this is more crucial if we have a touch of old-age diabetes, as most of us finally develop. To those of us who're still reasonably healthy but have come to the age when circulation, especially to the toes, has begun to decline, it's now necessary to stop taking your feet for granted. Feet, on an aged frame, must be carefully protected against cuts and bruises because toes take increasingly longer time to heal. Some sores don't ever heal.

This is no problem for the landbound since we rarely wander about shoeless on land. But bare feet are the most common mode on the deck of a boat, where there's a veritable forest of places to abuse toes. Stub a bare toe against a deck fitting and you could open a cut that may never close, and the pain could last forever.

Farewell to the carefree barefoot days of our youth. Your feet must be protected. Sandals are no good since they leave your toes out inviting abuse. Socks don't protect much and usually land you on your ass on a slippery deck. Good boat shoes with white soles or comfortable sneakers must be worn at all times. There's no excuse for not guarding your feet against the endless bumps and protrusions of your deck. Lack of toe protection can end your sailing days faster than a heart attack, not to mention missing out on the last dance.

In addition to toes, your feet themselves must be safeguarded. For your entire life the few square inches of the soles of your feet have borne pounding by the entire weight of your body. As you age, your feet begin to show wear and tear. The problem is that if your feet go, you might well be looking at a wheelchair.

To protect your feet, retrain your upper body to take as much weight as possible. Build a strong arm and shoulder musculature that can be used to take some weight off your feet. Practice moving about your boat with *no* weight on your feet by using only the lift of arms and shoulders.

Your tired old feet will be grateful.

Made in the Shade

If you're still lithe enough to twist around and get a good look at your ancient backside, you'll be delighted to discover that you have the ass of a baby.

This is because only your ass, and its front part, have never been exposed to the searing rays of Old Sol. Sol is the age maker and the source of skin cancers that can easily kill those of us who, as sailors do, spend a considerable amount of time outdoors. And if we don't die of the sun we blotch up in a most unsightly manner.

Our skin is the largest organ of our body. It's the first line of defense against the myriad of organisms that seek to do us the dirty. Our skin is remarkably efficient in warding off infections, but it's equally remarkably inefficient in protecting us from sunlight.

There are two kinds of epidermis: Epidermis Fragilus and Epidermis Asbestos. The lighter skin offers no protection, but African skin, over the millennia, has built an almost impenetrable genetic barrier to the killing rays. Since most sailors are whiteys, and since we're incapable of thickening and pigmenting our skins, it's necessary to interdict these killing rays.

First, be very, very wary of claims of so-called sunblock concoctions. The sunblock sellers measure the "effectiveness" of their creams by providing a numerical ratio. For example, in the United States, sunblock 15 allegedly equates 15 hours of sunlight to have the effect of one hour when the cream is used (European sunblocks use a different formula). What you're not told is that the tests are made under very special conditions; to wit, the cream is applied very thickly and isn't rubbed in, and nothing is allowed to wipe it away during the test. Also, water is banned . . . including sweat and tears . . . not very promising for sailors.

Sunblocks may make you feel protected, but in real life they make matters worse if you mistakenly allow yourself to add more hours of abuse. The bottom line is reapply sunblock thickly every two hours. Below the bottom line, do not depend on sunblock: wear clothing.

Protecting your body is reasonably easy and comfortable. Clothe yourself with light but opaque fabrics. My all-time best choice for protection from the waist down is a floor-length muumuu (see more about muumuus on page 148). But protecting your head, which sticks out like a lightning rod in a thunderstorm, is another matter. A cap with a visor does nothing to shield the back of your neck and only occasionally protects a protruding proboscis or high and sexy cheekbones. A hat is better than nothing, but make sure that there's a voluminous flap covering your neck and that the visor itself is huge to the point of ridiculous.

Then there's the problem of reflected light. The sunlight that is reflected off the surface of the water comes up at you from below, at an angle for which your hat gives no protection. The only total protection for both reflected and direct sunlight on your face would be a veil of see-through material hanging from the visor to below your chin.

There's plenty of this kind of material available, but no one, to my knowledge, has put two and two together to ban both kinds of abusive sunlight.

You'll have to do it yourself.

Don't forget your awning!

Pain and Comfort

An elderly gentleman stepped off the curb and was knocked off his feet by a passing car. The driver leaped out in dismay; attempting to ease the shock a bit, he rolled up his coat and put it as a pillow under the man's head.

"Are you comfortable?" the driver inquired.

"I make a living," the old man replied with a shrug.

Comfort is different strokes to different folks. Historically it meant "assisting," as in aid and comfort to the enemy. In recent times it's come to mean comfort in the sense of physical ease. Comfort for the rich is different than for the poor. Comfort for the young is wildly different than comfort for the old.

Comfort on a sailboat is as close to an oxymoron as one can reasonably get. There just is no comfort in a small vessel in almost any kind of seaway. There may be high excitement and intense pleasure, but *comfort* is simply not a word that we associate with the rewards that sailing gives us.

Young folk with smooth, tight muscles and uncreaky joints deplete more of their body's capital when at sea than they would on land. A young animal has this reservoir of energy to expend, and indeed, using up physical capital is part of the business of being young. Young animals have little need for comfort, or else there would be no contact sports.

We old folk have already used up much of our reserves of physicality. When an old body, lacking capability, is presented with a physical challenge, it seeks comfort.

Logically, therefore, the last place that an old bod should be found is on a sailboat. We sailors aren't all mad, at least not entirely (except in the opinion of landlubbers), so if we're to sail, we must redefine *comfort* not in the pleasure of an act but in the lack of pain. Everything we do in our sailing life must be thoughtfully and passionately anti-pain.

The best way I know to reduce pain is to reduce velocity. The first velocity to reduce is the forward motion of your vessel. The slower you go, the more stately your progress, and the less chance that some errant piece of boat will sneak up and whomp you on the ass. Anything over 5 knots is an act of arrogance for which we pay in the end or in some other soft part of us.

As boat speed increases, the activities required to control her ratchet up exponentially. This means that you must leap across the cockpit, rather than slowly scrunch over, to handle line or wheel. The leap can cause a break, a wrench, or a bruise, none of which is easily dealt with by a vintage frame.

Slow down. Develop a magisterial sailing style. Emulate the tortoise, for in truth you're already decades ahead of the hares.

Pace should be moderate, measured, leisurely, and un-hurried both in hull speed in the sea and in your own speed inside your hull. Velocity kills . . . a bullet traveling a foot a sec-ond won't even bruise.

At sea it's best to be a very slow bullet.

There are other places where pain can be minimized for antique physiques. The most important is in the head of your boat. The business end of a head, the toilet enclosure, should be just tight enough into which to squeeze. It's best that elbows touch and brace against its sides and that the door to the head be close enough upon which to lean your weary head. The most comfort that I've ever had during evacuation at sea is when, braced side by side against the weaving of the boat, I can put my forehead against the door and take the twenty-pound weight of my head off my neck. Then the real business can begin.

Toileting comforts are serious matters for old men who may not retain the free flow of their youth. Peeing, for reluctant urinary tracts, requires patience, time, and concentration, so all small comforts are to be considered. They aren't called com-fort stations for nothing.

Because of the intricate geometry of sailboats, bunks are surrounded on three sides by walls. Making up a sailor's bunk requires the degree of elasticity of a fourteen-year-old gym-nast. The older you get the less likely it is that the bunk will be made up.

Abandon tucking in the bedding. Fold sheets and blankets atop the bed. In cold weather you could use a sleeping bag, but remember that bags require agility from which to emerge, and if you're an old sailor, emerge you will several times a night.

Anti-pain in the cockpit requires a lee corner liberal with the softness of cushions. Anti-pain in the galley requires oilcloth, full-length aprons, and straps to keep you outboard of the stove and away from the splatter of hot oils. Anti-pain on deck is an oxymoron. When your boat is trying to abuse you in a heavy sea, get down on your hands and knees and crawl like a baby. This position is also advantageous for prayer in exigent circumstances.

Anti-pain in a companionway ladder is one so designed that you can bump, when things get rough, your ancient bottom unceremoniously up and down the steps.

Great pain and distress are generated when going onboard and offboard your vessel. Gangways, if they exist at all, are usually poorly thought out. My own worst moment was with a ladder used as a gangway. One foot went ahead of a rung and the other behind it, and I crashed down onto my most precious jewels.

The very best place for an old salt to be on a boat is at the navigation station. Build one with extreme consideration of support and brace in anticipation of quick naps so beloved by us old guys. The nav station is the one place on a vessel where the skipper can spend endless, guiltless hours in intense "navigation" without being suspected of shirking, malingering, or snoozing.

The lesson that we learn as we sail into terminal decades is that a sailboat is the least pleasant place to be, except for all the other possible places to be. The lesson learned is that comfort isn't, nor should it be, the aim of the sailor, or indeed, of life itself.

There is, however, a delicious obverse to the vexing discomfort of sailing. In the midst of the batterings and thrashings, any small comfort that might come your way—such as a warm mug of hot chocolate or an extra ten minutes in your bunk—generates prodigious pleasure.

Indeed, how else to measure pleasure than in the mitigation of pain? (See more on comfort beginning on page 253.)

A Killing Experience

There's a spot in the Pacific Ocean that's more distant from land than anywhere else on the globe. Two thousand miles to the east are the mysterious Galápagos. Two thousand miles to the west are the glorious Marquesas and the Dangerous Archipelago. It's even more than two thousand miles to the north and south before any land is reached. The loneliness is palpable.

It was here ("approximately," as a good navigator adds) that I, approaching my seventh decade, had my killing experience. The nearest reachable port where medical help was available was two thousand miles downwind, about eighteen days away. I would have been dead long before eighteen days had passed.

Ignorance aside and luck always to be wished for, a sailor's survival depends on having at hand resources, information, and initiative. I survived my killing experience because we had the medical resources on board, we were able to get the information we needed (via amateur radio), and we were blessed with a woman with the initiative to put it all together.

The morning was splendid. We were running easily down the trades toward Tahiti. The sea, the winds, a fine boat, and a remarkable woman conspired to make that morning one of the best of my life. I lazed aft, bemused by the morning, naked, as we always are at sea in the tropics, and disinclined to break the spell. In this mood I ignored my own orders to wear the clammy oilcloth apron used for protection against burns when using the stove.

I had opted for an alcohol-primed kerosene stove because of its safety, to which everyone also attested, and because everyone said kerosene was the most available fuel in strange ports. Nothing is so likely to be false than that universally held to be true. Both kerosene and the priming fuel, alcohol, are difficult to find, and lulled by everyone's assertion that kerosene is the safest fuel, I allowed the moment of carelessness that led to my killing experience. That which is most obviously safe can easily become the most dangerous. I'm learning to distrust familiar stuff. Like the friendly bathtub, it's where killing can happen.

Kerosene can be made to burn only after it's vaporized by igniting a bit of alcohol around the burner. It's a Rube Goldberg process, but it works well when you're tied to the dock after a good night's sleep ashore. It's difficult to judge the correct amount of alcohol required. The alcohol frequently burns off before the kerosene is vaporized, and you're left with a hot burner that must be allowed to cool before the process can be repeated. Waiting in a galley at sea is not anyone's favorite activity, and it becomes habit to give a little extra squirt of alcohol at the hot burner. With luck, which is most of the time, you get a poof of hot air, and the process gets started again. It's a chance we all take, a chance that can kill.

It's a chance I took, bare naked and with too little experience with burns. The stream of alcohol ignited and flamed back up to the bottle in my hand. The bottle ignited, and as I threw it from me, it bounced off the sink, turned lazily in the air, and sprayed me from haunch to fetlock with burning alcohol. I charged up out of the galley, the floor of which was blue with flame, as were both of my legs. Later the lady said I looked like a shish kebab; she added with womanly priority, "that was better than a weenie roast."

She grabbed a pillow, smothered the flames, and in the same motion doused my legs with water from a jug kept, for no good reason, by the sink. This was a lifesaver since burns continue to "cook" even after the flames are extinguished. The water cools the skin and halts the burning process. Much trauma was avoided by the cool water, but I was left with second-degree burns serious enough to kill. If the shock doesn't kill you, infection will.

Providence or pure luck now wrote a lifesaving scenario of coincidence. Years previously my son and his wife and I were on a summer daysail on a chartered boat in a quiet little bay in the south of England. We were about an hour out (downwind), and he had gone below to make tea. I had the tiller, and stupidly, without alerting him, I tacked about. The water he was boiling spilled over his legs. He sustained second-degree burns, eerily identical to those I suffered five years later. He quickly went into shock. We had to get him help fast, but the quick run out with the wind became an aggravatingly slow beat back. We almost lost him.

Later, after completing his medical studies, my son made up a medical kit for my Pacific crossing. Remembering his own terrible burns, he made the prevention of shock his first priority, so codeine came aboard. Next was the prevention of infection. In his accident, shock could have killed him, but since the hospital was only hours away, infection couldn't. But he realized that when you're far at sea, the need to control infection for days, or even for weeks, has to be considered. An antibiotic was, of course, the answer. But on a small boat, where immobilization is impossible and where motion endlessly abrades even healthy skin, a regimen other than bandages was needed. Nothing until that time had been developed to address these conditions.

Providentially, there was a product that deals elegantly with burns in the uncontrolled environment of a pitching, crowded boat. Silvadene, a sulfa-impregnated silver oxide cream, acts as an analogue bandage and provides all the security of a sterile antibiotic without the terrible consequences of the application of cloth to naked, burned tissue.

In preparation for our transpacific passage, my son placed a large jar of Silvadene in my kit. Later that same day, acting on a compulsion he could not explain, he added four more. He had no way of anticipating that there'd be the need to control the deadly threat of infection from burns covering 20 percent of my body for eighteen days, but the providential voice spoke, and the other huge jars were stowed. One jar would have killed me as effectively as no jars. Now there were five.

We had codeine and Silvadene, but we knew little about their use. Missing was still the professional information needed to begin effective treatment. A perfect solution would have been to have a physician on board. Failing that there was amateur radio. There's not one moment, day or night, anywhere in the world, that I can't call into effective operation a responsive network of ham radio operators. As soon after the accident as I could, within minutes before the pain took hold, I told the crew to reach out on 14.313 megahertz and seek aid.

There's a peculiar, conservative, and altogether admirable tradition among sailors that one never calls "Mayday" save in overwhelming threat to life and ship. I found it impossible to give the order for Mayday. "Call Medical Emergency," I said, "and keep calling until someone answers." The microphone was taken by another shipmate, Cyndee, a woman with a great pair of lungs, who soon made the first tentative contact with a ham net. The net operator, in Texas, cleared the frequency of all traffic, and across the whole world the only voices to be heard were our weak one from the mid-Pacific and those of the capable and experienced hams who took over my emergency.

"What can we do?" they asked, and I, illogically, insisted that they locate my son working 7,000 miles away in a Philadelphia hospital. I trusted and valued his knowledge, and most importantly, he had put my medical kit together and already knew what resources we had on board. There were several physicians on the net (there always are), but I wanted my son, so they set out to find him. Within half an hour Gil was on the radio, relayed via Texas. Gil already had the Burn Center in Philadelphia waiting on another line.

After that, all was anticlimax. I had codeine. I had Silvadene. I had loving care and instantaneously radioed medical advice. Eighteen days later we fetched Hiva Oa in the Marquesas and consulted a doctor at the little local clinic, who declared me cured. Healed with no infection and practically no scars.

I was lucky. Learn from my luck. Each time you untie from your dock, old friend, act as if you'll be a thousand miles from land. Think through all eventualities, no matter how improbable the scenarios seem. Seek out the experts and the physicians, seek out the sailors who've been there. For as sure as

God made little apples, you'll someday find yourself in need, and the killing experiences of others may save you from one of your own.

We had one serious shortage. Our cotton bandages for holding the Silvadene lightly to the burns were used up in a week. As I watched my lady tear linen into strips, my mind wandered, reality blurred, and for one brief and glorious moment I, Rhett Butler, lay injured watching a daring Scarlet O'Hara pull a petticoat from beneath her skirts and . . .

Remembering

Upon visiting an old couple celebrating their fiftieth wedding anniversary, their friend noticed that the old husband constantly addressed his wife in terms of endearment. Honey, Sweetheart, Darling, and My Precious were some of the loving names the husband used.

The visitor couldn't help but comment on how wonderful it was that, after all these years of marriage, there was so much demonstrated affection.

"Yes, we've been happily married for half a century," the old guy replied, "but about ten years ago I forgot her name."

The normal way memory seems to work is that we recall exactly things that happened decades ago, but we tend to forget matters that occurred a mere five days, five hours, or even five minutes ago.

The good news is that we all learned our important sailing skills in our distant past. These skills are engrained into our brain and muscles and will stay with us forever. Red right returning . . . red sky at night . . . the dangerous quadrant . . . and a thousand other snippets of how to sail will never leave us.

However, the question remains how to deal with short-term memory or with new skills that are only recently learned. The bad news is that most of us, or at least I, can't hold onto those ephemera. My real past starts some years ago, and all the stuff since I either must write down or depend on a younger head to remember.

My wife is my short-term memory. Without embarrassment I turn to her for the instant piece of info that I might require. I'm not afraid to say "What?" or "How?" or even "Who?" upon meeting folk from a few days ago who remind me of nothing at all.

The trick is to accept short-term memory loss as simply part of the hand that's dealt and to treat it much like the diminution of vision and hearing that comes with age. Besides, there are blessedly fewer things that a sailor *must* remember at sea compared to the myriad instructions and warnings confronting us on land. There's little else in this world as simple and as undemanding as the operation of a sailboat. Instructions absorbed, and rigorously followed, are as immutable as are the requirements of the sea itself. There are no shifting, amorphous, situational requirements at sea. Rules learned, techniques mastered, and processes understood have no deceit in them at sea.

The Ultimate Antidepressant

If you're an old sailor, the only kind of depression you're ever likely to fall into is of the barometric variety. The saving grace of falling into a barometric depression is that you'll be too busy to even dream of falling into a depression of the psychological variety.

Meeting a depressed old sailor is as unlikely as meeting a fat old sailor. In addition to shedding fat, old sailors shed guilt, boredom, irrelevance, and low self-esteem. This is the baggage that bedevils old folk on land and makes the last third of our lives hardly worth living.

Papa Hemingway fell into a depression and introduced himself to the business end of a shotgun. His is the exception that lends credence to the rule. Hemingway was an ardent fisherman, and fishing, like sailing, is a pursuit that generates more emotional satisfaction than fish and can go on until the weight of a pole with a ten-pound line tilts the old fisherman gratefully overboard. But something, perhaps Hemingway's heightened sense of the dramatic, caused even this great mind to give in to depression.

There are many pleasant things in life to which one can yield. Depression isn't one of them. Giving in to depression, especially in old age, is the road to death by either one's own hand or one's own mind.

There's nothing that must be battled more assiduously by old folk than that wasteland of gray depression that sucks meaning out of those activities that are still open to aged bodies.

In my own life, depression has been held at bay by two obsessions. The first is a small talent for writing, and the second is a huge need to go to sea. Even the writing palls at times, but the urge to be asea in a small vessel never has.

At the helm of my own sailing vessel, which puts no limits on my ancient itch for newness and adventure, it's been impossible for me to lose the sense of my own worth. Even when I've been held ashore for too long, my tethered vessel reminds me of vast oceans crossed and invites me onward to others. Sailing is the bottomless pit of experience.

The ultimate charm of sailing your own vessel is that you become the absolute center of the universe. You accept the satisfying responsibility for your own survival. You pit your skills and knowledge against an adversary that cannot be defeated yet allows endless and delicious small victories that are the ultimate stuff of satisfaction. The ultimate small victory and a great life lesson is when you finally accept that sailing a straight line may not be the shortest route toward where your life is headed.

Old sailors simply don't have the luxury for self-indulgence nor for the cloying indulgences of others. Old sailors don't have the time for boredom, busy as we are with line, canvas, and route making, and the endless task of keeping the sea outside our hull.

And at the end of all the small victories offered to old sailors is the quiet, secure, and delicious sense of self-worth.

Pumping Blood

Old bodies tend to develop restricted circulation, especially in extremities. Restriction leads to leg cramps, usually at night when heart rate slows down. Cramps appear especially after old legs are called upon to do Herculean work, as on a sailboat.

The usual treatment for a leg cramp is to "walk it off." Walking out a cramp works because the pumping action of lower-body muscles sends blood into the cramping parts. This is great advice on land but not likely to be of much use in the confines of a sailboat, where "walking the plank" may be a bit too draconian a cure.

The simple answer is to use your gluteus maximus muscles (the muscles of the *butt* or *ass* in common parlance) as pumps to send blood down the legs. Clenching and releasing these massive muscles can be accomplished without getting out of your bunk, and anyway, you'd have no place else to go.

Without awakening the rest of the crew, the clench-release will ease the pain, which, if you haven't yet experienced it, can be impressive. Getting out of a bunk in the confines of a small boat in the best of circumstances is a difficult task, so curing a leg cramp while still abed is a solution. It is, anyway, much preferred to the climbing and heaving, even without a cramp, involved in disentangling yourself from the confines of a sailboat bunk.

One of the problems with cramping is that the abuse to a leg muscle as a direct result of a cramp is "remembered" by the muscle, and an ache, rather than a powerful pain, can be felt for a long time. The "memory" lasts well beyond the pain or the ache, and continued abuse will lead to repetitions of cramping in *exactly* the same location.

Leg cramping is endemic for old legs, whether sea legs or otherwise. Both at sea and on land cramping is related to the general condition of your health and your arterial distribution system. An old sailor, while calling on his legs for more activity than does his couch-ensconced cousin, will be in better shape, and his cramps will diminish, if his body is kept active.

It's one more really good reason to keep sailing.

Idle Thoughts

The Green Flash

Rare is the Green Flash,
The Sun's 'goodnight'
By which day is concluded,
Occluded
By Earth's rim.

Evenascent,
Momentary,
Transient,
So ephemeral that
Non believers argue its existance.

I have seen the Green Flash
Deep in the Pacific
Two Thousand miles deep.
Believe me, the Green Flash needs only
Your belief.

Reese on Bill's Committment

Consider this about Bill Pinkney:
He had no money.
He had never sailed in a deep ocean.
He is totally deaf in one ear.
He comes from a broken family.
He was raised on welfare.
He is Black.
And, Lord help him, he is Jewish.

At the age of fifty, when most men are dickering for cemetery plots, Bill decided to sail solo around the world via the canals. At fifty-two, Bill altered his plan. The new plan was to sail solo via the five capes.

Sailors have done this before, but no one has ever approached this daunting program with Bill's particular package of poverty and lack of experience. Being Black and Jewish might not be considered detriments to a circumnavigation, but when you consider the state of the world, they sure aren't advantages. Unless you're Bill Pinkney.

Bill Pinkney, born on the seamy South Side of Chicago, educated only to high school, clawed his way out of two ghettos to become a successful Yuppie marketing type. He joined a middle-class synagogue, which found his blackness intriguing. In his job he found himself enmeshed in a community of adept Great Lakes sailors, all white and few Jewish. Bill had to be the best marketer in Revlon, the best worshipper in his congregation, the best sailor on the racing committee, and the best Black in the local NAACP.

In retrospect, considering the pressures and demands that such a life program put on Bill's baldy, grizzled head, all these confrontations might not be such a bad preparation for taking a 47-foot sailboat alone around Cape Horn. Bill took to sailing on the Great Lakes with the verve the envy of all who knew—or knew of—him. At the very least the prospect of getting out alone and putting all that emotionally, intellectually, and racially debilitating conglutination behind him must have seemed to Bill to be a kind of heaven and not the hell that a solo circumnavigation evokes in most sailors' minds.

Peter Vanadia, who ran a true sailors' boatyard along the Delaware River in Philadelphia, called me one afternoon. He heard I was back from sailing and insisted I meet Bill when he arrived that week to ready his boat. Saturday my son called to tell me that I must come down to the yard. This, said my son, was my kind of guy.

The boat was on the trailer, having just arrived overland from Chicago. She had been violently introduced to a bridge abutment that had torn out some starboard lifelines, bent the steering pedestal, and committed sundry other indignities that a lady in a hurry really didn't need. Her name was *Commitment*. He was going to do it. The long voyage of finance and preparation, of wheedling and coaxing, and the battle with self when time after time he lost heart, were over. This other long voyage seemed at that moment to be an Elysian escape.

Bill Pinkney stood by *Commitment*, a little lost. His dream, crouched on a trailer waiting to be tamed, was very real in front of him. As with all dreams and wishes, the moment comes when your best and worst fears are realized. The arrival of *Commitment* at the shore of the Delaware, in smelling distance of the open sea, brought home to Bill the reality of his prideful intent.

Bill may be Jewish, but that makes him no less Black, so he opted to make a statement for those other Black kids who, for lack of patterning, would spin out their time in poverty and drugs in the ghettos of Chicago.

Bill had been that rare animal, a breed just emerging in America, a black Yuppie. Having made the team and joined the club, he found that the thrill of achievement dribbled out, and a haunt of questions troubled him. Was the success game worth the candle? Was the rest of his life to be a replay, a dull déjà vu, of the time till now? Bill said no and cast about for a challenge with meaning, for a chance to do what no other Black had done before him. He would sail, solo, around the world—and give to the culture from which he had sprung a genuine, imitable hero. Bill Pinkney was finding his true relevance in his approaching old age.

Now commenced a series of events both bizarre and unplanned. The Good Lord had in store for Bill dramatic twistings that even Hollywood might reject.

When Bill came out of high school with no money for college, he joined the navy as a pharmacist's mate and served alongside, as the fates would have it, Bill Cosby. They kept in touch some over the years, and when both Bills turned fiftyish, Pinkney confided his dream to Cosby. He didn't ask Cosby for assistance, but Cosby passed the wild plan along to Armand Hammer.

The plan had now transmogrified more into a desire to raise the spirits of dispirited Black kids than the sailing itself. The sailing, the enormous solo effort, fell into the background as first Cosby, then Hammer, and then others twanged to Pinkney's impassioned plucking. Without the commitment to the kids, Cosby wouldn't have listened; without Cosby's urging, Hammer would never have taken the bait and, eventually, would not have been able to get the temporary loan of the great circumnavigating boat belonging to Mark Schrader of solo world-circling fame.

There lies deep in the hearts of those who can a stream of pity or guilt for those who can't. Cosby, Hammer, Schrader, and, finally, three others poles apart in Boston succumbed to Bill Pinkney and succumbed to the kids.

Pinkney, conspiring with Margaret Harrigan of the Chicago school system, came up with a computer-satellite program that allowed the kids from the South Side, bound up in close cityscapes rather than distant horizons, to follow his progress daily. The computer program expanded to include all sorts of information relative to the precise spot on the globe in which *Commitment* happened to be sailing. The kids were charged up with the adventure of the Black sailor alone on the sea. Many accepted the implication that they could do it, too.

It was a very difficult program to resist, even for three proper Bostonians—who prefer to remain nameless—who shelled out $300,000, thereby giving Bill the glorious opportunity to put himself seriously in harm's way.

Commitment arrived at the Delaware sans paint, sans supplies, sans steering, and sans a lot of other stuff with only a week to go. Most of Bill's free time between New York and Cape Horn was taken up doing all the stuff that was left undone when he sailed off from Philadelphia. Bill was busy.

Mark Schrader really made it all possible when he allowed Bill to have the boat for the three and a half years that it took to raise the money to buy it. Mark says he extended Bill's option to purchase "two hundred times," and after three years the money finally appeared. Mark's interest, and his patience, go back to his own involvement in a school for disabled kids. He knew what Bill's program could mean to the kids on the South Side.

Mark also empathized with Bill over the agony of the major wheedle that Bill was going through. Telling the same tale of need over and over again was something that Mark had already been through, and that experience, and the benefit to the kids, caused Mark and his partners to wait years for money that might otherwise have come to them in months.

I spent a week with Bill in Philadelphia just before he pushed off, unready and untested. I watched his calm patience crumble in the face of unnecessary emotional imposts and the dragged-along baggage of years of convincing other people of his dream. He began to yearn for the loneliness of the sea, and suddenly the mystery of why solo sailors do it became a bit clearer for me.

Solo had, for Bill Pinkney, become not a challenge, as it's usually described, but a salvation. Escape from the madding crowd is possible for only a lucky few who are eager to trade the impossibilities of dealing with the world for the impossibilities of the lonesome sea.

Bill's paean, like Martin Luther King Jr.'s, drifts back down onto the grimy streets under Chicago's El, or elevated trains: "Free at last, free at last, thank God Almighty, we're free at last."

Rummaging Life

I recently rummaged my boat for the first time since she was launched in 1979. At that time she was a lighthearted lass, showing a naked boot stripe and a bit more of her roundy bottom than was deemed altogether proper.

She was something of a hussy in her salad days, holding her skirts high above the tickling seas. She was a frisky one . . . before I laded her from fear that there would be no chandlery in the South China Sea. For China is where we were going, not exactly consciously, since sailorly destinations are rarely planned . . . they just seem to happen.

Twenty years and 30,000 sea miles later her bottom had disappeared in matronly skirts and her boot stripe was, perforce, raised lest it be lost entirely.

When I finally rummaged, I watched with delight as first her original boot stripe appeared, and then, tantalizingly, her cute and sexy bottom peeked ever higher out of the water as she was unburdened of decades of mostly useless stuff.

Up out of the holds came steel cable, unused and unusable, and tools of heroic sizes more fitting for a nuclear sub than a lithesome pleasure boat. There was an entire nest of hundreds of heavy glass jars of peas bought in excessive quantities because of price in Romania. The peas were uneaten since Romanian pea quality matched Romanian pea price. Discovered were a wind generator, never used, and a massive wind vane laid aside when my autopilot appeared. The generator was heavy steel, and the vane was heavier bronze; *Unlikely* purred a bit as they were hauled ashore.

It could be argued that an excessive number of anchors is prudent for far places, but . . . nine anchors! That was prudence carried to the extreme, especially since they were inextricably deep in the hold and permanently and uselessly entangled in hundredweights of ancient rusting chain.

There were more miles of hawsers to protect against typhoons of Eastern seas. There were sails, still folded as they came from the sailmaker, of such arcane application that I'd long since forgotten their use. And line and screws and bolts and a wash of washers and extra stanchions and even one complete 12-foot, 300-pound, stainless steel spare drive shaft.

As I aged, along with my vessel, my waistline expanded to accommodate more unneeded pounds just as *Unlikely* was accommodating to ever more unneeded tonnage. She and I, bloating our waistline and waterline, shortened our useful lives as we accumulated useless poundage.

If I were to continue to sail, and it was unthinkable that I wouldn't, the fat had to go. But the rummaging of one's own body isn't easily undertaken. There are so many temptations ashore. It was not until my heart cried "enough" and sent me a shattering warning that rummaging my body became first an imperative and then an obsession. You really can't lose weight unless you become obsessed with the process.

Rummaging requires that *everything* be off-loaded onto a dock, looked at, and judged for usefulness. On the dock it becomes obvious what was useful and what wasn't. Only what's absolutely useful is reboarded. Pleasure isn't a consideration. First shape down the vessel; then, and only then, may pleasurable matters be considered.

Rummaging your body works the same way. The best way to rummage your body is to set out on a long ocean passage. Most oceans can be crossed in a month, give or take a few days. On a long sail three things promote the delarding of your gut: the temptations of land don't exist on sea; it's intimidatingly difficult to prepare a meal at sea; and for some of the time you'll be seasick, or at least sea queasy, a most effective mechanism for eating less.

This is why old sailors are lithe and bony. And, in the very final analysis, perhaps this is why thin old sailors are old.

Passing Time

The second question everyone asks when you tell them that you're just back from a month at sea is, "Don't you get bored?"

(The first question is, "Don't you get seasick?" To this you answer that you never get seasick. That is, of course, a lie.)

The boredom question is, by far, the more interesting. What *do* we do with all those great dollops of time in a long passage? Indeed, what do we do with all that time we spend aboard tied to our dock? This is time in which there's little, if any, intrusion from the real world. Time that's uniquely our own. How do we use it? This is a particularly germane question for those of us on the downward slopes of sixty and a crucial question for retirees.

Boredom happens to old folk when we have nothing that we *must* do. Nothing like that can happen to a sailor. There's *always* something that must be done, and more likely than not you're the only one to do it.

As you think back over your own long passages, you rarely have any sense of what you actually did. You know that you weren't bored. You know that you changed sails (not often on a long passage). In the current state of the art of sailing almost no one is slave to the helm (let Autopilot Man do it) or to geography (let GPS Man do it).

There are crucial activities that are so natural in the context of sailing that you hardly remember doing them. There are chores that you'd never do at home, but that need doing aboard ship, and you're elected.

Where does the time go?

Cleaning

Much time is spent in cleaning—a despised pursuit at home for a respectable old fellow, but somehow attractive when it involves your beloved boat or a piece of your expensive equipment.

Personally, I enjoy most of all that intense, finicky, and un-necessary energy expended on cleaning objects that really don't need cleaning. I adore, and perhaps you do, too, digging out tiny bits of crud embedded deep in seams, which do no harm to any-thing. I'll work endlessly with a pointy ice pick to remove de-posits that are perhaps better left in situ or, at least, aren't worth the time and concentration required for extirpation. When that little elusive bit of debris is finally worked out of its hiding place, I get an inarguable thrill of achievement. Don't you?

At home I sometimes deign to dry dishes but rarely, in my glorious maleness, to wash them. Washing dishes on a leap-ing, tumbling sailboat, with no washer lady around, is a time-consuming, expert, and energetic pursuit. You wash and care-fully protect each fragile dish against the concentrated intent of your boat to fling them willy-nilly about the galley. How much time does that pass? A guess: if it takes ten minutes to wash dishes in the quiet stability of your kitchen, it takes half an hour for each meal at sea. So there's an hour and a half gone from the day in dishwashing alone.

The cabin soles must be scrubbed and degreased (half hour) lest you land ignominiously on your butt, spills must be cleaned up (half hour) and, of course, you must scrub yourself.

Bathing is a problem and requires a personal decision about grooming. A half-shaven, bedraggled, and smelly old skipper hardly inspires confidence. His crew imitates him, and soon the boat is as unappetizing as a bucket of swill left in the sun. But it takes time and effort to bring even a semblance of landlubberly elegance to a working sailor. Shaving with a razor? Slow work. Dangerous work. Perhaps that's why so many old salts are bearded.

In the matter of clothing, sailors old and young have three options: 1) Stink. 2) Bring enough to last the whole passage (but where to store?). 3) Do your own wash. Another hour a day shot.

The cleaning of equipment can use up your whole life. I know a lady who scrubs her running rigging and mooring and docking lines once a week with detergent and bleach till they become soft as a baby's behind. She claims this task gives her enormous satisfaction, but it costs her a couple of hours.

Airing bedding, drying and desalting sheets and pillow-cases, putting them back on the bunks—all take time.

Personally, I like to clean my engine. It doesn't run any better; indeed, sometimes it runs worse, since I invariably manage to dislodge a wire or a coupling as I bumble about in the bilge. But I love getting all that nice grease off the engine and onto me. (Which then involves more time to get the grease off me.)

Need I go on? Make a list of all the stuff you clean on your boat, and next time a landlubberly type asks if you get bored, ask him when was the last time he degreased *his* engine.

Putting Stuff Away

Any little job on a boat usually involves hauling out and sorting through everything that you've neatly (and compactly) stowed away. By the time you've finished your little fifteen-minute job (which usually takes three hours), you're faced with the depressing task of restowing your entire boat.

My guess is that after decades of accumulation I spend a couple of hours a day just restowing everything from pots and pans to butane torches to line that needs reflaking and to reclaiming that damned wrench (the important one) that has insinuated itself once more into the filthy bilgewater. (Which involves more time to get the filthy bilgewater off me.)

Cooking

This depends on how well you want to eat. Old sailors soon learn that the search for variety uses up old and limited energies. Best to set a healthy regimen and repeat it with only a few variations throughout the passage. Cold food works since cooking involves an intense hour of isotonic tai chi to keep hot stuff from sliding into the bilge or into your lap. By the time you've healthfully reached the advanced age that you are, you've learned, or should have learned, what foods do you the least damage and the most good. Take that hard-earned knowledge aboard with you.

Getting the stuff to the table unspilled requires sixteen arms since you're now spread between galley and table. The smooth and slippery table perversely shoots your agonizingly prepared dishes onto the upholstery as soon as you set them down. Before the days of stabilizers aboard ocean liners, the stewards, in rough weather, would simply toss a pitcher of water on the tablecloth. Works better than Velcro.

Bilge Time

I've spent more time in the bilge fussing with my engine than in any other activity aboard. I'm often tempted to emulate those few old salts who tear out the devil by its steel roots and fling it over the side into the convenient deep. Tempted, yes, but I'm not quite as brave as they are.

Almost any job, at the start, seems like a fifteen-minute job. The truth is that all engine jobs take a minimum of three hours, although not many extend—thank the Lord—to more than twenty hours. Once you're into the engine, there's no possibility of backing out. A disassembled engine is an imperative, a slave master that brooks no mañanas. In my last long passage we were working in the bilge for no fewer than ten days, two of which were spent tearing the boat apart (and another day putting it together) in search of a six-month-old leak in our freshwater system. We spent the rest of the time remounting a fridge compressor, resiting an alternator, and so on ad infinitum and ad nausea.

On the average, we all spend 20 percent of our sailing time scraping our tortured knuckles and breaking our old backs in the impossible confines of the engine compartment. This may include the time spent repairing radios, self-steering gear, running rigging, antennas, winches, windlasses. The list is endless.

To all this must be added the time to install new equipment and improve old installations, which you've foolishly left to do en route. I spent two days installing a water-tank-level meter during my last passage, and then the damn thing didn't work anyway.

Time for You . . . Reading, Daydreaming, and Teaching

Then there are the activities that you delayed during your working years and have saved for "retirement." Pursuits not encroached upon by your boat. Pursuits denied you on land by the stentorian calls of day-to-day events.

You've brought aboard all those wonderful books that you've cravenly ignored in your middle years. "I'll read them on the passage," you promise yourself. When you get off a cold watch and snuggle down into a warm, dry bunk with a long-ignored book, your mind may say "read," but your body says "sleep." The battle is won by your body. After a few pages the book drops on your chest, and you're off to the land of dreams.

Speaking of dreams, a major onboard activity is daydreaming, which, old friend, is why you've found yourself on a sailing boat a thousand miles from shore. Somewhere in your early life you "dreamed" yourself there.

I daydream endlessly about my next boat (every sailor's dream), the distant Pacific Islands, the sweet South Atlantic, and all the passages I've yet to make. I dream of the really serious book I'll write some day. I dream of how extraordinary, wonderful, delicious this passage is. All this dreaming takes time.

Old skippers spend much time teaching. A sailor is made by hands-on experience under the eye of someone who's been through it before. There's no other way to become a sailor. My first "offshore passage" was from Miami to the Bahamas, 90 miles that seemed to me like 900. I'd asked an experienced skipper to sail with me, and he taught me dead reckoning, without which you can't call yourself a sailor. I spend much time en route teaching navigation, knots, and other know-how, but I always start with dead reckoning. It's incredible how few young sailors can do it, enslaved as they are by GPS.

Teaching is time best spent. Sharing your experience with novices enriches not only their lives but your own as well.

Time for Love

With a little luck, there's no upper age at which making love comes to an end. For some poor folk it stops at thirty or perhaps never even starts. I know eighty- and ninety-year-olds who still rise regularly to the occasion. Health aside, it can be argued that given the time and the exclusion of the world's importunities, love can happen at any age.

Where, where in all the world, where in any setting, in any clime, in any condition, can lovemaking be better than in the otherworldly privacy of your own boat in a quiet anchorage? Where better than afloat in a translucent sea over a smooth and sandy bottom? Isn't this the absolutely proper setting to address yourself to another, softer, smoother bottom?

When have you and your love had the leisure to really investigate each other? Have you ever had the endless time it takes to painstakingly please your mate? Where else can you hear the promising burble of warm water around you to encourage your own burbles? Where else do you have the encouragement of nakedness and the erotic browning of sun-warmed bodies? Only on a vessel in your own private cove. Call your vessel *Eden*, for that's truly what she is.

Sans relatives, sans neighbors, sans kids, pets, knocks on the door, sans telephone calls from the office, sans the wasteland of television, for whose phony eroticism you can now substitute the real stuff. If you're an old guy or gal who's let slip out of your life this central joyousness, then here, out of the sight of a judgmental society, you may unself-consciously relearn its delights.

As you consider the many-faceted uses of time on a sailboat, certainly that which benefits most from the special ambience of sailing is lovemaking—leisurely, uninterrupted, unhurried, diligent, heedful, exhaustive, and exhausting lovemaking.

When the next time some landlubber asks you how you spend your time aboard, ask him when the last time was he had eight uninterrupted hours to make love to his lady.

(Or better yet, if you have a really nasty streak, ask his lady.)

Naked We Came

Your aged body is nicer than you think.

On land the unfeeling folk about you will believe that the old body you hide under all those clothes is too terrible to view. 'Tain't so. An old body has *character;* it speaks of your decades of battle with the world; it is, indeed, a sort of decoration in itself. Whatever you've still got . . . flaunt it.

There's this delicious feeling of freedom that infuses us when we find our old selves bare-assed alfresco. Everything flips and flops about in a joyous dance of release. When every other body around is at least as funny (beautiful) looking as ours, we relearn the precious lesson that there's nothing—physical, emotional, or spiritual—that makes us so all-fired different from everybody else. Saggy can be sexy and droopy can be delicious when we realize with delight that there are few perfect nymphs other than those attenuated models manufactured in Hollywood. Naked, we rejoin the human race, and if you happen to be a man in love, there's no need for passionate declaration . . . your affection, rising to the occasion.

The problem is to find someplace to be naked without attracting a drool of overdraped weirdoes. Nude beaches are full of sneaky peepers; besides, sand is a crevice-seeking substance that can be damned uncomfortable where it counts. You could shed in your own back yard, but that lacks the requisite sense of adventure. You might try Main Street, but your bare butt is likely to be tossed in the cooler. Very uncomfortable.

My best place to be defoliated is on my sailboat, where my audience is of my own choosing and as weird (no more, no less) as I. On my lovely vessel we can barely (pardon the expression) contain ourselves till we're out of the harbor to fling vestments aside and, once undressed, regain contact with air and sun and sea and, now and then, with each other. How simple it all seems and how free. With the molting goes not only damp drapery but all the other ties that bind on land. Along with clothing the suspicions and trepidations of crowded land may be dumped into the sea. Sans clothing, dissemblance is difficult. Not worth the effort.

Few are so lucky to have a sailboat on which to escape into a controlled ambience. Not too many old guys have this perfect opportunity. All the more reason to get a boat.

There are occasions, even asea, when we have to settle for some sort of cover-up, but don't despair. There's something that's almost as good as nothing, that even works when your children, your harshest critics who would squirm at your sartorial absence, come to visit.

Nearest to being naked is to wear a muumuu, often referred to as a sarong. A muumuu is nothing more than two square yards of cotton cloth. It is donned, either above the breasts or below, by either sex, with a quick wrapping motion followed by a few folds and a little tuck. It's the best, the easiest, the most informal, the most or least revealing, and—not to be sneered at—the cheapest, habiliment available to our species. It needs no tailoring, no letting in or out with vagabond waistlines. It defeats obsolescence and requires no keeping up with the Joneses. It also serves as a sunshade, a towel, or a considerate cover for a delicate derriere presented by the two-backed beast to the sun if such matters, devoutly wished for, should come to pass.

The muumuu has another unequaled, enchanting quality. It's infinitely variable, according to the wearer's personality. Jaunty? Tie it low. Sexy? Show some thigh. Demure? High under the arms. Cautious? A knot in place of a tuck. Fashionable? Fold a pleat at the tuck. Athletic? Pull the tail through the legs and tuck into the waist. Bashful? Wear two. Shameless? Fold once, then wrap. And so forth and so forth.

There's no personality nuance to which a muumuu won't be amenable. It matches and enhances the infinite variety of the human psyche as well as providing a delitescent veil for those aged parts of you that you can't yet bring yourself to make public.

The muumuu is the Esperanto of attire, the bête noir of high fashion. Cheap, beautiful, and infinitely variable, it allows

you to be as naked as is reasonable in the presence of your un-
closest friends.

It's the Declaration of Sartorial Independence.

*Detailed directions for making a muumuu: Obtain a piece of cloth
one yard wide and two yards long. That's all, folks.*

Wheedle, Haggle, and Mooch

By unprincipled use of wheedle, haggle, and mooch, the cost of cruising for us old folk can be dramatically reduced while we luxuriate in that delicious feeling of beating the system. "Pride goeth before your bankroll," to sharpen an old saw. Like most attitudes carried to extreme, pride is expensive, especially for us retirees whose funds have become limited but whose passions for sailing toward far horizons have not.

If you're as old as I am, you remember the Hippie 'Sixties. The lesson learned then was that a lot of folk can exist very well on what our rich economy lets fall through the cracks. To benefit, at the max, from these manna-like droppings, you must first be in a position, both emotionally and physically, to gather in the goodies.

Getting your old hands on throwaway sailorly stuff is what I'm talking about. Since *old* is synonymous with *poor* in our confabulated society, we elders start out with an impressive advantage in the world of wheedle, haggle, and mooch. Our poverty requires no establishment; our white hair is the only proof we need to engender a sentimental desire to help in those who think they have more than we.

Getting free stuff is only part of it. There's also shameless haggling, tax dodging, and getting the best of a barter. All in all, not the sort of advice you're likely to get from prideful sailing magazines that push the empty concept that sailing is mostly a matter of looking better than your neighbors. The real trick is to look *worse* than your neighbors, in which condition your neighbors, driven by *their* excessive pride, will rush to cast their treasures upon poor old you.

An American in a foreign country, at the mercy of a language not fully understood, is not considered a normal human being. We're pocketbooks with dollar signs for eyes, and should we appear a bit doddery, we're considered an easy mark. The merchant's job is to take you. Your job is to save whatever dollars you can and thus extend your sailing range a bit more.

Whatever price is asked, offer one third. You'll be met by scornful looks of rejection, but the seller will realize you're either a hard buyer or just plain stupid. In either case, the seller is now aware that taking your money won't be easy. Dollar signs fade in his eyes as the haggling begins.

There's no such thing as offering too little. You can always magnanimously raise your bid a bit, but you can *never* come down. Remember that you never know what the merchant's real price is, nor do you know at what point he'll roll over.

My father, of blessed memory, told this tale in teaching me to haggle. A new immigrant, a greenie as they were then called, was sent off to Jake the tailor to buy a new suit for the Sabbath. He was advised that whatever price Jake the tailor asked, the greenie was to offer half. The bargaining started at $100, for which the greenie offered $50. An hour of haggling, and the price was $30, for which the greenie offered $15.

And so on until, in disgust and exhaustion, Jake the tailor screamed, "I can't stand it any more; take the cursed suit for nothing and get out of here."

To this the greenie replied simply, "No."

"What do you mean, no? I said take the suit for nothing."

"No," said the greenie, "I want two suits."

Another tale, this time true, occurred some years ago, before I started my passages. Strolling in Philadelphia, a friend of mine and I entered Rittenhouse Square, where we espied an absolutely stunning girl sauntering along the path. My friend went up to her and, without so much as a how-do-you-do, said, "Would you like to sleep with me?" The lady hauled off and delivered a tremendous slap to my friend's face and stalked away in high dudgeon.

I was aghast. I remonstrated with my friend. "You can't do that. You can't simply go up to a woman and put such a question. You'll certainly get slapped."

With a secret smile my friend said, "Yes, yes, I know. I get slapped a lot." With this he paused, and his smile broadened a bit as he continued, "but sometimes, not often, but sometimes, I get lucky."

It's the same with haggling. Sometimes, if you're tough enough, you walk away with a great treasure. Come to think of it, the same is true with life. Even the Bible says, "Ask and you shall receive."

On coming into a new port, a "poor old sailor" on a poor-looking boat has two options: to anchor out in the protected waters of the port at no cost or to go to dock in the most expensive marina he can find. It's at an expensive dock next to profligate boats that the opportunities appear.

Here's how it's done. Wait for Friday to go into the marina. Pay for a three-day stay. (You'll stay for four, but marinas never go to the trouble of collecting for the last day since you unexpectedly develop "engine trouble.")

Every marina has spaces reserved for the charter fleets, and you must insist on a berth on the charterer's dock. You drape your rigging with old rags, hang out objectionable laundry, smear up your pristine white work with mud, and scatter a lot of frayed lines about.

You've chosen Friday because that's the day that all charters end. As they return, look as old and as frail as you can as you help with their lines. Let them know how jealous you are of their glorious boat and ask if perhaps they can let you buy their surplus food (they failed to anticipate inevitable seasickness).

The riches are astounding. Charterers, unaccustomed to stocking a boat and intent on the best that money can buy (since food is only a small part of the cost), acquire too much food that's too rich and too expensive. Generally, since they have absolutely no use for the surplus, they just leave it aboard. You, in your demonstrable poverty, give them the opportunity to feel generous and magnanimous at no cost to themselves. Your offer to buy food will be refused. A hundred times out of a hundred they'll *give* you the stuff.

From just one such encounter with charter boats, we've walked away with supplies for three months. It's well worth the insignificant cost of three days' berthing.

But why three days if all the charter action is on Friday? Because the weekend is when owners with permanent berths come to work on their boats. Marina-based owners, wastrels all, take great pleasure in throwing away marvelous stuff to make room for stuff no more marvelous but slightly newer.

Police the trash cans on Saturday and Sunday. Watch for tools, chain, stainless fittings, blocks, line, bumpers, oil from oil changes (perfectly OK in an emergency since profligate boats change oil too often), upholstery, even in one case a perfectly good GPS that had been judged not automatic enough. One lucky Saturday morning I found a kicker with lines frayed and useless but complete with blocks and stainless fittings, worth about $200, tossed cavalierly into the trash. Another time a beautiful, undamaged stainless bow pulpit. Its value to build: about $1,000. I can't imagine why it was disposed of.

Profligate boats don't repair anything. If it doesn't work, the hired skipper, as uncaring of the boatowner's money as is the owner himself, trashes perfectly repairable stuff. Gather it in and repair it at your leisure. At the least, if it duplicates what you have aboard, you can trade it off with another poor boat.

I was once given a lovely little two-man rubber assault boat by some Russian friends who had, in the resulting confusion after the breakup of the USSR, liberated it from the Russian army.

I had absolutely no use for it, but the sailor on a neighboring small boat saw it and lusted after it. The rubber boat fit his needs. In exchange he offered me a brand-new navigational computer that he had bought and never used because he was almost never out of sight of land. The swap was made to the intense delight of both parties.

The moral: Accumulate, whether you need the stuff or not. Somewhere, sometime you'll profit.

Finally, never, never pay excise taxes (value-added taxes) since sellers pandemically cheat their governments and keep the tax for themselves. When you have haggled down to the best price you can, simply refuse to pay the tax. At this moment the seller, having invested heavily in energy and time to make a deal, envisions all his effort wasted if he refuses. He'll probably roll over.

For those of you who might feel demeaned by such tactics or who think the haggle, wheedle, and mooch approach is below your sense of self, let me tell you a true story about a Very Rich Person and how he got his start.

After the war (my war, the Second World War) this VRP who then was not yet Very Rich, offered to buy an Atlantic City hotel that had been used as a hospital by the army. The absentee owners didn't have the faintest idea of what to do with their property and were delighted that they had a fish on the line. The negotiations (haggling) began. They ran for over a year with a dozen lawyers involved on the sellers' side busily running up enormous hourly charges. The VRP had no lawyers involved and didn't care how long the negotiations dragged on. The sellers were impatient and lusted to get their hands on the cash.

Finally, after eighteen months and hundreds of thousands of dollars in lawyer's fees and with the sellers frantic and exhausted, a deal was agreed upon. The price was to be $5 million in cash, and the VRP agreed to a settlement date when he was to appear with the money.

The day came, and the lawyers, now swelled to thirty, convened expensively. The sellers, convinced that the fish was in their net and that the deal, even after deducting the lawyers' fees, was very attractive for them, were rubbing their hands in anticipation.

Our VRP sat down at the table and coolly announced. "Gentlemen, I know that I agreed on a price of $5 million, all cash, but, sadly, all I have is $200,000. The rest I'll owe and pay you out. Take it or leave it."

You can imagine the consternation. You can imagine the name-calling. But after tallying up their enormous legal costs and lacking the stamina to go through another battle with another buyer, if there indeed was one, the owners took the deal. Our VRP had his first, of many, hotels.

Our VRP went on from this, his first mooch, to become one of the richest men in America. If not being afraid of what "they" think of him was good for one of the richest men in America, it's good enough, my poor old sailor friend, for you.

Beat the System

The only way that old salts can survive nicely is to figure out how to beat the system. Most of us made our retirement money when income and prices were low. Now, thirty years later, the system has so ratcheted up that our carefully husbanded resources shrink to inconsequentiality.

One of the advantages of being old is that in trying to save money for really important stuff you're judged as being frugal rather than demeaned as being cheap. You no longer need to keep up with anyone but yourself, and you suddenly find there are wonderful alternatives to the blandishments of hucksters.

With the leisure of a retiree and some careful thought, you'll come to see that there's little on your sailboat that can't be found cheaper than at the boatyard or the marine store. Since dollars to us old types become scarce with our exit from the economic fray, we must develop "cheap" into a fine art.

Actually, beating the system is dead easy as most of the monster-priced marine stuff is designed for folk who equate price with value, an act of high stupidity.

This thought was thrust upon me when, in perusing a sailing magazine, I spotted the latest offering of an anchor that guaranteed easy release from the bottom. Interesting . . . until I saw that it was for a mushroom anchor, which is about as useful to a real sailor as bosoms on a bull. What really got my dander up was the price, $249 for a mostly unhelpful mushroom anchor that should go for about $30. But it had a gimmick.

The gimmick was an extra line that went down into the shank of the anchor and released the flukes when tugged. I was about to inform the "inventor" that a piece of line, a trip line for about a dollar, attached at the bottom of the mushroom, would do the same job, when I saw a quote from him.

"There is money in anchors," he chortled without embarrassment. You bet there is, I felt like replying.

Actually, I'm indebted to this fellow because he started me thinking about all the passionately promoted products that do little more for old sailors than lighten their already thin retirement wallets.

Here are a few of the more egregious multibuck extractors to which I append simple methods to avoid these devices.

Replace a $250 Prop Brake for 35¢

One of the universal mysteries of sailing is that when you're under sail a freely rotating prop causes more resistance than one that's been stopped. To accomplish the stopping, dozens of eager folk (eager to separate you from your moolah) offer highly engineered, really cool-looking "propeller brakes." Not only are they expensive, but they're difficult to install properly even by the mechanic that you hire at $40 an hour. Thus you can add $100 or so to the approximately $250 the brake costs. That comes to $350. I can build, install, and operate a prop stopper in sixty seconds for 35 cents.

Here's how: attach 2 feet of light nylon line to a strong member near your prop shaft. Wind it three or four times around the shaft *in the direction of its rotation.* You can now stop your prop with a slight two-finger tug on the line and keep it stopped by tying the line to anything nearby.

Avoid a $100 Exterminator for 50¢

At some time or other every boat hosts cockroaches. These wee beasties don't eat much, but at least in my case, they taketh away my appetite. There's simply no reason for any sailboat to be burdened with a cockroach supercargo. If they want to go somewhere, let them take a bus.

Upon sighting a roach (the nonsmoking kind), you raise a great flap as you charge about with a rolled-up newspaper. In most cases, since they're very fast, you miss. A friend of mine, a passionate despiser of insects, once got so riled up that he successfully got the little bugger with a well-placed .22-caliber shot. As the well-placed shot was placed below his waterline, he had some other problems with which to deal.

If you spray cockroaches, they die in a satisfying manner where they're doused. But you accomplish nothing about ridding your ship of the thousands hidden in the hold and the thousands more eggs just waiting to hatch and terrorize your wife.

Cockroaches have a very annoying habit of developing a resistance to normal chemical sprays. The ones that don't die go on to multiply happily . . . unhappily for you.

What is needed is 1) a method to which they can't develop a resistance; 2) a method that doesn't kill them until they get back to the nest; and 3) a poison that doesn't do away with your cat.

If you've ever washed your eyes with boric acid, you used, in powder form, the magic Kockroach Killer. Boric acid powder sprinkled about is guaranteed to make you totally cockroach free and *to keep you in that blessed condition.*

It really isn't magic. It's not even chemistry . . . it's more like physics. The little buggers love boric acid, which they ingest, and then they wander back to the nest. Nothing much happens until a thirst descends upon them, and they drink, at which point the boric acid absorbs the moisture and simply explodes its hosts. The exploded gents are then eaten by their friends in the nest who, in their turn, explode and so forth and so forth.

I know of no insect that can breed a resistance to an internal explosion. Nor do I know of many killer chemicals that will do the dirty to your roaches but won't harm your canary.

Boric acid powder may well be the means by which human beings outsurvive cockroaches in the distant future.

Spend $3 on PVC and Save $$$

To save yourself hundreds of dollars, buy a couple feet of 4-inch diameter PVC pipe. Slice it into 1-inch sections. Screw pairs to your pilothouse ceiling. Roll (do not fold) your charts and insert.

Who needs expensive chart drawers? Besides, you use space that's useless for anything else.

"Mother Trucker to Ancient Mariner": Two-Way Radio for Embarrassingly Little

If you'd like two-way, onboard radio, and your vessel is less than a mile long, there exists a wonderful substitute for short-range high-frequency handheld units at $400 the pop.

Citizens band radio is one of those technologies that had a screaming success and then simply died because it was so successful that no one could be heard over the raucous. Nobody uses CB radio anymore, which means that we old guys, ever respectful of antique technologies, can check out any yard sale or pawn shop where old handheld CB radios can be had for a song. A cheap song.

When you're at sea, CB frequencies are free of the interference that still makes them annoying on land. Should you go abroad, most countries of the paranoid variety ban CBs for the locals altogether, so you have the luxury of keeping in touch with your crew on shore leave as they wander about strange and wonderful native marketplaces.

The cost is usually whatever you offer. Nobody wants the things.

Buy a Little Pocket Compass for $3 and Save $400 on Binoculars

One of the more outrageous extravagances that are urged on sailors is the insistence that a pair of binoculars for $400 is ten times as good as a pair for $40 because it contains a $3 pocket compass that acts as a sighting compass and because the manufacturer says it's better. But the story gets better.

Some time ago I won (I surely wouldn't buy) a pair of multi-hundred-dollar binoculars on a bet with a friend. At the same time I invested about $40 on a pair of the cheapest binoculars I could find. I discovered that there was the minutest visual improvement in the expensive pair over the cheapie and that the resistance to salt spray is about the same in both. Both withstand about a year of hard use before they begin to dim out and before the aluminum housing starts to go.

When my super-duper pair went belly up, I checked with the manufacturer and was told that $100 was the very *least* it would cost to repair them. Since that would give me only about another year of use . . . I saw the light.

I got smart and deep-sixed the old $40 pair, spent another $40 on a new pair, and relegated the high-priced pair to a yard sale at which some poor fellow thought that he was getting the bargain of his life for $100.

I now buy a new pair of el cheapo binoculars every year. At that rate I get new binoculars for ten years at the same cost that one pair of the high-priced version would be.

Oh yes, don't let anyone tell you that the nifty looking rubber armor that adds to the cost is much good against salt.

How to Pay $0 Rather Than $314.95 for EPIRB Replacement Batteries

Replacing an EPIRB battery usually involves the time to "return to the factory" and lots of dollars. There will be occasions when time isn't available, and anyway, the question of cost is always important.

Old EPIRBs are really nifty to have as a backup when you trade up to the next generation 406 series. But it can cost $100 or so to repower even an old-generation EPIRB.

To avoid shelling out $100, all you have to do is remove the old battery (which must be done anyway) and use the leads to wire the EPIRB directly into your boat batteries. An EPIRB wired thusly will be powered as long as your boat batteries last.

Replacing the battery for the 406 model also involves "return to the factory," and the cost, as quoted by ACR, is $314.95. Wow. Like the older models, the 406 can also be wired to your boat batteries in an emergency or if the EPIRB drains its own battery. ACR technicians confirmed that the 406 is a 12-volt machine and will work perfectly well on your boat's 12-volt batteries.

A caveat: In both cases you lose the portability of the EPIRB, so if you anticipate very long passages and foresee taking to your emergency life raft, wiring the EPIRB to your boat deprives you of an important facet of the EPIRB system.

How to Get Two Years of Antifouling for $14, Thus Saving $1,400

Some years ago I began to use a cheap additive to my antifouling paints. For fifteen years I've been enjoying the blessings of longer periods between haulings and the nifty feeling that I'm contributing less than I would have to the pollution of the seas by minimizing my use of metal-based paints.

The Abusive Bottom Paint Problem
First abuse: Bottom paints work this way. You put metallic-based antifouling paint on your boat's bottom. Small animals attach themselves to the hull and ingest the metallic poisons. They die and drop off. The metal in their bodies then goes into other animals and ultimately into solution in the sea. Do this enough times, and you get a serious pollution problem.

Second abuse: The incredible price of antifouling paints. You need not only a costly hauling but also outrageously expensive paint. Antifouling paint usually lasts for three years, so the estimated cost *per year* to protect your bottom for an average waterline can be as high as $700 per year, and maybe higher.

Clearly, if the length of protection of antifouling paint can be extended, the savings are enormous.

The $14 Solution
Sidle up to your friendly pharmacists and get some 500-milligram capsules of tetracycline. Open one capsule and dump the contents into a liter of antifouling paint of your choice (the cheaper the better). Stir well and apply. The tetracycline extends the life of antifouling paints by at least an additional two years.

How it works: The presence of tetracycline prevents the formation of "sea slime," which is the necessary precursor to the attachment of barnacles and similar animals. Without the slime, animals can't attach to the hull. Thus the sea is saved from the abuse of two extra years of metal pollution. Since tetracycline is an easily broken-down compound, what does get into the sea does minimal harm.

Thus you save $1,400, which you would have had to pay after three years since now you have five-year protection. And you did a good, "green" thing.

A Final Word about Money

Money is always a big concern for old salts. Our salaries are long since past us, and our savings suffer from the endless attrition of the market. We must substitute craftiness for cash. Rather than money, we must suggest our advanced age as payment.

When all else fails, offer a seller half his asking price and remark, "Look, I'm old, cheap, and cranky."

For some reason this convulses most folk, and you walk away with your treasure.

The Let Syndrome

I have a kid brother, also a sailor, now approaching his seventh decade, who had a terrible time as a child. He was so asthmatic that our mother would stay up nights nudging him back to life when it became too much effort for him to breathe.

He grew up deep in a miasma of pity from four loving aunts, a distraught mother, and grandparents who would gladly have spent their lives running and fetching and carrying for the poor sick child.

But the child would have none of it. He was far too young to understand that this deluge of assistance would simply cripple him, yet he somehow understood. The very first word that ever emerged from him, laboring through the whistles and rales of his asthma, was "Seph!" We all soon came to understand "seph" meant that this weak-lunged, strong-willed child wanted to do it, whatever it was, him*self*.

He understood better than his healthier siblings that chronic illness attacks more, much more, than the body. It attacks the will to combat illness itself. Tasks and decisions and activities are ceded over to too willing hands. His debility could have destroyed him and sucked out of him the glorious poetry that he was to write as he came of age. He came of age . . . doing it all "seph!"

A debility such as severe and chronic asthma is not dissimilar to the debility of age . . . in both there's the disinclination to add the strain of activity to the discomfort of illness. As we age, everything becomes incrementally more difficult. The threshold of discomfort descends as your age ascends until, should you allow it, almost everything is being done for you not because you can't do for yourself but because it hurts a little and you're surrounded by a loving clan who are deep into the Let Syndrome.

The insidious Let Syndrome starts out innocently enough. "Here, let me help you with your coat," or "Oh, let it be. I'll clean up later." The Let Syndrome becomes the process by which you're entwined and immobilized in a soft and "loving" web, a web that, should you allow it, robs you like a thief in the night, taking first your purpose and soon enough your own sense of relevance. If, after all, you let others do the things for you that are a shade more convenient for them to do than for you to do yourself, your image in their eyes becomes one of an aged, incompetent, and disabled creature whose only remaining relevance, in their eyes, is the slightly comforting feeling they might get when doing something "nice" for you.

However, the inconvenience of serving you soon overcomes whatever little pleasure there is in the serving. Love becomes impatience and ultimately turns to the dismaying realization of how much you're disorienting their lives.

Never mind that they constructed the restricting palings around you. Never mind that they've continued and extended the process so that your own personal space has painfully constricted, and never mind that, in the whole disgusting process, they're diminishing your quality of life by discouraging life-enhancing activity. Ultimately they encourage your enfeeblement, thereby reducing the number of reasonably pleasant years left for you.

Do not, old friend, "let" anyone do anything for you. It will be enough that you'll "let" them carry your coffin to your grave. It's simply not acceptable to "let" you repose as if in your coffin while you're still alive, as they bustle officiously about you.

We old folk must accept the twinges and aches that we've honorably earned. They are the anti-rewards, but rewards nevertheless, of years spent in service to the cabal now circling about you, denying you the sometimes unpleasant but sometimes surprising amusements of simply being old.

If you're an old sailor, the pressure to allow assistance can be overwhelming. The normal limits of age are magnified exponentially by the tossing about that an old body suffers from being at sea. It's so easy to allow someone else to cook or to bring up a cup of coffee or to shorten the sometimes agonizing hours of a late night watch. On land the effort to lift your old bones out of a chair to get for yourself is merely uncomfortable. At sea, with every muscle and tendon straining to fight the rollick of wind and waves, the effort to disallow assistance becomes an act of heroism. However, the rewards of maintaining your relevance are also heroic.

So long as you can physically haul your poor self about, you *must* continue to do so. Any backsliding toward hands offering comfort, toward folk chanting the desolate mantra "Let me help you," will steal away yet one more shred of your shrinking self-respect.

So long as you can continue to shuffle about on your own, you'll delay the moment when you'll be obliged to shuffle off. Your future stretches out so long as you hold tight to the reins of your life. Drop the reins, and you're a dead man.

Do not "let" them shorten that future.

Like my kid brother, you must shout, petulantly if need be, to anyone offering a helping hand, "Buzz off buster . . . I can still do it 'seph'!"

The Sailing Mariness

Muse

The many Uses of Muses
(Such as this one)
Amuses me.
Oh Well.
Chacun a son *Muse.*

Elizabeth Pearce on the Gifts of the Sailing Life

With my eightieth birthday beckoning weeks away, the inclination is to blink and ask, "Who, me?" Sure, the mirror, that liar, shows an old woman where my image ought to be. Certain parts of me have become somewhat high maintenance. Still, a light aerobic workout five mornings a week and walking a couple of miles a day help keep the body machinery working.

I live alone in an apartment overlooking a tranquil bay and marina, entertain family and friends often, drive a lot, buy e-tickets on-line, and travel by air several times a year. The past two years as president of SSCA, a 10,000-member international cruising organization, required a considerable amount of administrative duty. In addition, I administer two family trusts and am personal representative for an estate that is the plaintiff in a lawsuit. It's doubtful I would have had physical and emotional energy to meet these demands without the years spent at sea. They afforded a quality of environment seldom available to those living on land. I believe they extended my life.

Over forty years ago I took up sailing because it looked like fun (it was), and I wanted to see if I could do it (I could). After raising two children and having a twenty-five-year career in public relations, I sailed offshore with a partner in a boat we owned together. The partner wearied of the demands of a small boat and went ashore, selling his half of the vessel to me. He wanted to be with grandchildren and enjoy another lifestyle.

I continued on, remaining offshore nearly fifteen years and living aboard twenty-one years.

A small sailboat at sea is a prime venue for a healthful lifestyle. There's pure, fresh water from the rain-catcher or a reverse-osmosis system; clean, sweet air in abundance; simple, nutritious food and plenty of exercise—aerobic, cardiopulmonary, and weights. Mental stimulation comes from solving mechanical problems, planning sailing strategy, evaluating weather data, and plotting navigation. For emotional health there's ample time for introspection and opportunity to gain self-knowledge. Intellectual growth comes with time to read and to explore others' minds through interaction with fellow cruisers and other cultures. As a bonus, there's neither road rage nor drive-by shooting. Little wonder then that one emerges with a strong, healthy body, mind, and spirit.

A couple of years ago tragedy struck my family, leaving behind relentless, overwhelming grief. I hove-to a bit, letting the maelstrom pass. For a time the burden seemed unbearable, then little by little empowering lessons learned on the deck of a small sailboat came to my rescue.

At sea I smile a lot. Sitting alone on watch, with the sea stretching to the horizon, I feel the presence of God and his might, and my soul smiles. Watching an albatross for days on end skim and soar a thousand miles from land, never resting, my heart smiles at her constancy. Welcoming a rain squall that brings water for the tank and bathes me clean and fresh, my whole body smiles. The countless stars, the order of the universe, a visiting school of dolphins, a blue sky dotted with fair-weather clouds, all bring a smile.

Less contemplative times bring satisfaction of another kind. Equipment failures, inclement weather, contrary wind or seas all must be addressed. Whether one succeeds or fails at making a repair, whether wind and sea require heaving-to, whether you drop the sextant or the GPS fails, one way or another you deal with it, and when it's over, you smile within because you know more about yourself than before and because you survived.

—*Elizabeth Pearce, 2002*

Marilyn on Communicating with Your Mate

Living with a man isn't easy. This isn't a complaint, because I do love my husband. As a woman dealing with a man in a man's world, one must learn to communicate in a different, more secret, language.

On a sailboat there are special considerations. Both sexes must learn "boatspeak." No yelling. No abusive orders. No condescension. No pushing of emotional buttons. No manipulations. We're a team. For a successful passage, we trust, rely upon, and support each other.

There's no room for sexist behavior on a boat. We all do our share of *all* the tasks. Men can be wonderful in the galley and cleaning heads, just as women can be excellent navigators, using blind instinct rather than blind logic. Women have few ego problems in asking for information on how something works, how to get directions, how to adjust to discomfort. Men would rather get lost than seek help. This doesn't work on a sailboat. We're all interdependent. Toss ego overboard and just be equals. Partners.

Women are accommodators by nature. We negotiate to find a balance, whereas men tend to push their solution. With all the changes and challenges during a passage, emotions intensify. Women adjust to change much more so than do men, who might fight change. Women give in to emotions, thereby controlling them, while men seek, fecklessly and impatiently, to conquer them.

Patience is key to any passage. Instead of argument, we take the time to sit and discuss the experience whenever possible. If the situation calls for immediate response, the captain, male or female, must make the decision. Instructions are given, not barked. We've found that the "louder is wronger." Discussion after actions is important for understanding and for future emergencies.

I can hear his voice whispering, teaching, encouraging, inside my head as I go about my duties on the boat. Listening and focusing on an issue at the appropriate time is the best way to share a thought. Because Reese is dyslexic, I've learned that he must focus solely and directly on what I'm saying, or he tends not to "hear" me. Women can do several things at once, whereas most men—mine, at least—are singular in activity.

The core lesson I've taken from my years at sea with Reese is that watching and listening to him in the confines of a sailboat at sea, to the exclusion of the strident imposition of the voices of land, helped me see him more clearly as my life mate.

Unlikely is our universe. There's no place to hide or escape. No television, Internet, telephone. No hogging of the TV remote. No doors to slam shut. We deal with *all* issues or run the risk of disrupting a perfect voyage. We have the most rare opportunity to gain a closeness and bond in the rhythms and innermost thoughts of one another. We have the leisure and the clarity to share pure moments of quiet, glorious sunrises and sunsets, a school of dolphin off our bow, or just sitting in the cockpit during a star-filled night watch. My best advice to women is to share a few days without "outside civilization." Just you and your mate, some simple foods, a good book, quiet, and each other. From sailing, we've learned to pare down our lives, rejecting toxic people and the impudent cacophonies of daily life. We establish our own boundaries instead of allowing people to maneuver into our space. Sometimes I must be tough in setting rules. Reese has short-term memory of previous events and will try to push me against my instincts. Given time, we come to a mutual agreement. We don't use the phrase "I told you so."

Each time we set sail, I focus on a different challenge in the handling of *Unlikely*. From sail handling to dealing with officials, we take turns in the responsibilities. We know that the other has done the job. Teamwork.

As men age, their physical capacity alters. Age is no excuse *not* to do something. For us this means daily exercise and healthy eating. Exercise the body. Exercise the brain. I may call Reese "Poor Baby" when he's feeling poorly, but I'm relentless not to give in to his aging.

He's always said that I should drop him off the side into the welcoming sea when he can't be "alive and relevant."

We still have many sea miles to cover and some thousands of days to do so. Onward to new horizons together.

—Marilyn Arnold Palley, 2003

Marilyn on Sailing with Reese

Ever since my first taste of sailing back in 1975, when I was invited by a relative stranger to do a transatlantic voyage aboard his Westsail 32, sailing has dominated and expanded our lives. That we're still together, the "stranger" and I, through passages of oceans, seas, strange and distant ports, and a circumnavigation, is a tribute to sailing sanity and how it cements and expands bonds.

"How would you like an experience of a lifetime?" queried the voice on the telephone. As a twenty-two-year-old artist, I was game for anything. "Sure!"

The caller was one of my clients; he owned the gallery that had been selling my sculptures. He was worldly and experienced, being thirty years my senior. And he was a sailor.

Without much hesitation I was on the next flight to Senegal to join his crew. That I'd never been on a sailboat and never been to sea other than dipping my toes in the ocean along the beach never entered into my decision. That I'd lived alone and independently for three years and was claustrophobic also never entered into the equation. That I'd never spent more than half an hour with this man didn't matter. My friends and family had bets that I would fly back to the United States before ever leaving the dock.

The boat sat high in a cradle in the dock of the French navy in Senegal. It looked dwarfed next to looming freighters and fishing boats. Thirty-two feet would become my world as we finally set sail on *Unlikely V.* No one warned me about seasickness, or watches in the middle of the night, or the constant dampness and discomfort that quickly surrounded me. However, after three days, the world altered, cleared. The transformation from landlocked to ocean opened my horizon. I had gone through a sea change—my life would never be the same.

Being slapped in the face by a flying fish at night on my first watch, bleeding the air from an engine in rough seas, perching on a leaping bowsprit repairing a headsail, not to mention all the other learned chores and responsibilities, became part of this life-changing passage across the Atlantic Ocean. Each moment was special. I learned more about myself in those nineteen days than my entire previous twenty years. The passage set me on a new course for my future. When we called "land-ho" at Antigua, a sadness came over me that my journey had ended. But it was only beginning. Twenty-eight years and our circumnavigation later, Reese and I continue to share our lives on *Unlikely*.

"Captain of the ship" doesn't mean that Reese won't do any of the chores himself. As captain, he'll never ask crew to do something he wouldn't do. On land it's too easy to telephone a repairperson. When you're on a boat, self-reliance is key. I have fond memories of Reese on his knees, hands deep in muck, fixing the head.

The boat has taught me to check all the connections, follow a problem back to the source, make repairs that will hold up at sea until we get to a calm port, check and recheck repairs, check daily for water in the bilge and the water level in the engine and batteries, plot a course, and listen to variations in the sound of wind in sails, the engine, and any other pings and pangs one doesn't hear on land.

Captain is only a word. Reese and I are partners. We share in the chores and responsibilities. He's learned to listen and share in the problem solving. Our personal characteristics of the senses complement each other. My senses of smell, sight, and sound are highly acute and compensate for some of the burden of his decades. My attention to details, a female scanning and nesting instinct, is a balance to his male "hunting" of the bigger picture. Instead of fighting each other's capabilities for ego's sake, we accept and support each other. Sailing has given us special moments of emotional and experiential sharing.

As a food person, one of my jobs is to provision for our passages. Food should be fun *and* nutritional. Popcorn can be prepared a dozen different ways. Pasta is a staple we never grow tired of. Buying inventory for long passages in foreign ports has been a challenge. From Romania, when no canned goods were available, we carefully stowed glass jars of fresh stewed vegetables and fruits. There was no supermarket chain in Senegal, so locating canned goods was a scavenger hunt. In the middle of my first Atlantic crossing, I baked a pineapple upside-down cake for Reese's birthday. Creating meals becomes an integral part of the passage.

Six years and a heart attack ago, we bought a piece of land in the Florida Keys. It's on the water, where *Unlikely VII* could be docked by our home, ready to sail at any full moon. Then Hurricane Georges hit in 1998, and we spent the next three years rebuilding our beloved.

We set a date and began to make plans to sail toward Honduras to visit a friend and get some interior woodwork done before setting our horizon for another Atlantic Ocean passage hopefully in 2003. As we focused our energies on prepping the boat for the crew's arrival, everything else became secondary. The trip would be special as a sort of reunion of Marcus and Cyndee, who had been crew on *Unlikely* for five years, Reese's brother Norman, his nephew Brant, myself, and my husband, Reese, coming into his eighth decade. The nervousness that it had been six years since we'd sailed was a feeling that drifted away as soon as we hanked on the sails. With charts ready and larder full, we waited for the weather to alter for a safer passage. Local knowledge and weather predictions were for 10-15 knots in square seas through the Gulf Stream of the Yucatán Straits. Some boats had already returned to the marina damaged. We chose not to put ourselves or *Unlikely* through unnecessary confrontations.

Due to schedule commitments, the weather delay caused us to alter our passage and sail toward Cuba. We wouldn't do Honduras this trip. For me, migraine headaches hit for the next couple of days, so we decided that I should remain behind for some quiet time. Sunday morning I waved to them from the dock as *Unlikely* sailed out the channel off to sea.

The three of us—my husband, *Unlikely*, and I—hadn't been separated for more than a day for seven years. Now two-thirds of me was off and away, and I was alone. The days passed quickly as I kept myself busy. However, the nights were endless as I yearned to be on *Unlikely*. Sailing has been such a deep and natural part of my life for twenty-eight years that I can hardly conceive what life would've been without the sea.

Reese taught me that a sailor never says *to* but instead says *toward* for any passage, as anything could happen with boat, weather, time, or another port of call. On a sailboat, as in life, one must remain flexible in all matters.

That I didn't get to sail on the last passage to Cuba is something that won't happen again. I'm ready to take my favorite place on the leaping bowsprit as we head out to sea on our next passage. We'll sail toward our next horizon together.

—*Marilyn Arnold Palley, 2003*

Marilyn and I have been together, at sea and on land, for decades. When introduced to the sea she quickly became a capable, responsible (and decorative) able-bodied seaman. We're seen here in the Red Sea, she in her favorite faux leopard vest and me with somewhat more hair. As I lost hair and gained years, Mar, ever supportive, has kept me at sea. —*Reese*

Men Focus, Women Scan

There's a demonstrable difference between how men and women use their vision. This leads directly to the question of crew selection for old skippers.

All of us lose visual acuity as we age. The most common condition is a clouding of the lens that interferes with the clarity of an object being looked at directly.

Here's the problem. Men, because of their ancient aggressive biological construction, excel in the hunt. Hunting involves single-minded *focusing* on the future lunch. Focusing one's senses is an act of aggression, a condition at which men are peculiarly adept. Focusing, maleness, and aggression come together in the way that men act and see.

The problem for the old sailor is that clouding of the lens interferes more with vision precision than it does with the other archaic function of vision, which is to scan for danger and detect peripheral movement.

Sailors young and old have little need to focus at sea. At sea, we male sailors need primarily the ability to scan, a skill at which men are biologically diminished. Scanning is a maternal function in which the mother, all senses alert, scans for danger to her brood.

Men focus and women scan . . . so we have one more of the thousand good reasons to take on female crew. Over time women have become defensive in the "protection of the nest," and as a result, they're superb scanners. The act of scanning the horizon for distant trouble is the essence of good watchkeeping.

On watch, we've observed that men will quickly focus on one potential danger or condition and narrow their field of vision to the exclusion of other matters needing attention. Women on watch never narrow . . . they have a wide-ranging radarlike sense that was designed in distant millennia to alert them instantly to dangers to eggs and offspring.

Once in the broad and shallow mouth of the Yangtse River, the man at the wheel was so intent on maintaining the required distance from either shore that a freighter bearing down on us didn't register with him. The freighter was unballasted, and because she was in shallow water, she created a huge bow wave that, upon reaching us, put green water from bow to stern. When we discussed the event later, it was clear that the helmsman saw danger in the immediate need to keep water under our keel. His concentration was aimed at solving that immediate problem while the wider—and in his eyes less immediate—threat was missed. The problem was not only visual. He was also focused on problem solving, a typical male process. Women do not instinctively solve: they instinctively report.

Sign on a woman if only to protect you from distant dangers. In women, age is not so visually crucial as it is in men,

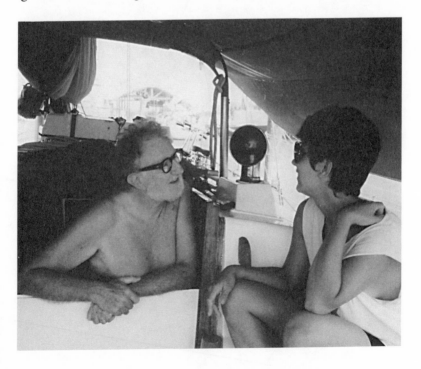

since clouding of the lens doesn't interfere crucially with peripheral vision. As we men age, we lose our most important visual capability and are left with a not very effective ability to scan. Women, even older women, retain those visual antennae that can protect you better than you can protect yourself.

Skipper, sign them up, put them on watch, and have yourself a good and carefree snooze.

Cautionary Tales

Chains

Separated
By twenty feet of land.
Unlikely on one side,
And I across the lawn.

We lean toward each other,
Unlikely and I,
Just out of reach
After twenty years of roaming.

The Sea sets Unlikely free.
My house imprisons me
With velvet chains of comfort.

Once before
I broke those chains.
But then I was much younger.

I met this iconoclastic analyst wandering about in the ocean of his release just as, much to his surprise, he gave up doing deep analysis in exchange for doing deep seas. Now two decades later, he's still at it.

—Reese

Don Weiner on the Gift of Clarity

Old Reese Palley had set me to what on the face of it seemed a simple task, to wit: unravel the emotional impact of a three-decade addiction to sailing on the life of a one-trick septuagenarian pony. Piece of cake, thought I. This mandate caught me just as I was about to depart for home from the Abacos.

My plan was to sail alone, spending a few flagrante delicto days with my 30-foot catboat while strolling at leisure through the gardens of my mind. But now this stroll had developed more purpose; it had become more of an analytical pilgrimage. Fun, I thought. Then impossible, I thought, a fool's mission to define a perfect sensual event. But maybe apocryphal.

Weatherwise we had the makings for a near-perfect passage, wonderful background music for my inwardly seeking stroll. Very soon my boat's singing, I'm in a sea cathedral, my heart's soaring, and this old agnostic is perfectly capable of prayer. I feel an enormous sense of beauty, correctness, harmony, and profound awe for the great mother and all the stuff she bequeathed to sailors. Over and over I marvel at the luck and privilege of a sailing game to play at seventy-one that somehow never seems to loose its luster or turn-on. I cherish this gift that gives such perspective. This gift so defines one's place that it makes letting go somehow easier.

The night creeps in. I'm alone in the axis of the Gulf Stream, in the axis of the universe. The sky is nearsighted Van Gogh. Thoughts are Thoreau. I'm filled with life, and it's a take-home message. It's a gold standard to stand against the pettiness, greed, hypocrisy, and narcissism, that endless list of human foibles. Nature plays no favorites, recognizes no guile. You can't fake it. She tolerates fools badly.

Amazingly, at times like these, feeling at the top of your game, you luckily get to take this homeostasis home. What a gift to the geriatric is this sense of clarity.

As you deal with your boat, it becomes a paradigm of how you deal with life. A mini-cosmos of your anxieties, dependencies, obsessions, lifestyles, and on and on. And all in a form pure enough to be understood by even those whose insight is challenged. A very good thing if you believe that the unanalyzed life is not worth living.

The night turns to "rosy-fingered dawn." It's been thirty hours since leaving. I'm very tired. Finally the flash of the sea buoy. Brilliant sunrise, a boisterous burst of dolphin greetings. I'm home. And I want to do it all over again.

—*Don Weiner, 2002*

Reese on
One Old Man Against the Gods

He was a furious old man, a man against the gods. Whether he held the Lord in higher disdain than his fellow men wasn't settled with his death.

Tristan died as he lived, far away from home in some part of the iconoclastic dream that was his life. He never

had a serene moment. Whatever good came to him arrived with a price, and the good, according to Tristan, wasn't worth the specie he traded it for.

The money by which he survived came from the books of sailorly dreams for which he was famous. Those who carp (and perhaps don't sail) argue in mean-spirited and disagreeably snobbish airs that all the adventures didn't happen, and if they did, these carpers snipe that Tristan added to and embellished what were essentially small events.

It's a dismal argument for a man about whom no one could ever use the term small. It was no small feat to wrench a mean living out of his quill. It was no small feat to leap over illness, to pass off the loss of one leg with a facetious name for his new vessel. It was even less a small feat to lose his other leg and with it the remaining ability to fend for himself.

For Tristan, fiercely independent as he was in thought, in deed, and in opinion, to have to accept the kindness of strangers in the last years of his life was the ultimate insult that the gods could have dealt him.

Those of us who sail and who dream and who find that our dreams are an improvement of reality reveled in the adventures of Tristan in which fantasy overleaped fact. In his books he let us join him in impossible adventures, just those adventures that we would wish for ourselves. Who cared what the fine balance was between fact and fiction?

That he sailed in the most difficult climes is fact. His confrontations and battles with petty officials were fact. How he bested them, how he turned impossible odds to great victories, are neither fact nor fiction. Tristan's battles against the odds, as he described over and over in his books, were little more than his irascible railing against the larger officialdom of fate.

I have two tales to tell about Tristan. Since I'm without his talent to swell small events into large confrontations, they'll be less interesting than he would have made them. But they're true and, even uninflated, they give the flavor of the man.

There came a time when I innocently sought to convert an ancient little harbor on the Black Sea built by Emperor Constantine into a modern Romanian marina. The project was beset by pettiness and obstacles, a process brought to a high art by the Romanians. In trying to deal with this I came to believe that only a Tristan Jones could smash through the barriers daily set upon us.

I asked him to come to Romania and be the commodore of the Constanza Yacht Club and the captain of the port. His job, which he accepted with an evil, joyous glint in his eye, was to whip these recalcitrant folk into shape.

He failed, but for a most curious reason.

He stormed into Romania on his one good leg and set about, as only he could, to make a silk purse. He spent the worst winter of his life in that small harbor, roaring up and down the docks in his wheelchair, spreading panic and terror. In the spring he confessed to me that, in spite of towering rages and brutal tantrums, the battle was lost. Since I'd seen him through worse times, I was curious to know how he'd failed to conquer mere men when he'd so often and so handily conquered the gods themselves.

"I'll tell you, boyo. The gods were easy. They stood and fought. The Romanians melt away at the first hint of conflict. It is like jousting with shadows. The worst enemy I never bested."

Years later when I left Romania, the memory of him was burned with the branding iron of fear into the sailors of Constanza. After Tris left Romania, I would go down to the harbor to look after my vessel, awkwardly stilted on the hard, and their mouths would whisper half in terror, half in awe, "Where is Captain Tristan?" but their eyes would be saying, "God grant that he never return."

The second tale about Tristan is a lesson in turning adversity into advantage. Tristan had more than his share of adversity, but he had the will and, being a reconstituted Welshman, the wit to turn the ill slings of fate back as if with a shield of Odysseus.

The place was the most flawed harbor that one could imagine. It's tiny, it's laced with ancient lost chains crisscrossing its bottom, and, worst of all, it's a magnet for every sailboat in the Mediterranean. It was entirely possible that summer day, with boats moored bow to stern, to walk across Rhodes Harbour dry-shod.

Tristan was there in the curious catboat that he'd built after losing his first leg. (When I once commented on his loss, he bellowed, "Dammit man, I didna' lose it, the bastards snatched it away from me.") The boat was built to allow him to haul himself about and provided numerous places where a one-legged man could wedge himself into a comfortable standing position. Tristan, who was known to take a drink now and now and then and then and then, opined that his boat would be a perfect pub, "no matter how drunk, or how few legs, she dinna' let me fall down."

He was leaving for a passage eastward, and since everyone in the harbor, especially the Brits and the Americans, knew Tristan, a cabal was formed to coordinate their boats' whistles, horns, and sirens at the moment Outward Leg (for that was the name chosen by Tristan) passed through the fabled gates of the Colossus.

The moment came. The English-speaking boats started to make a ruckus, and sensing something was up, the rest of the boats in the harbor of a hundred nationalities joined in.

The whooping and honking and sirening were impressive, and as Tristan slipped through the narrow entrance in full view of the world of his admirers, an event befell him that would have been seriously embarrassing to the greenest of sailors even at midnight in a deserted harbor.

He'd forgotten a trailing line that, at the moment of highest din, stopped Outward Leg dead in the entrance and pitched Tristan, who was at the moment waving in appreciation to the honor accorded him, flat on his back.

The harbor went dead quiet. It was hard to say who, the honorers or the honoree, was more embarrassed. Tristan's mate, a young Thai lad, was seen to slip over the side and emerge with the line in one hand and a mucky, dripping bundle in the other. Tristan, ever mindful of image, hollered over to those of us standing shamefacedly at the entrance.

"Never mind, mateys, the sea gods laughed today. They tangled my line onto the lost treasure of the Argonauts. I'll write about the treasure in my next book."

He never did, but the tension was eased by that Welshman's wit of his, be he Welshman or no, for some say that he rebirthed himself from England to Wales. Tristan had instantly come up with the perfect riposte.

What we now all have come to recognize is that the true Treasure of the Argonauts was Tristan Jones himself.

Errors and Commandments

I was installing a teak rubrail on my son's boat in Maryland when I caught sight of a Westsail 32 tied up across the harbor. My heart leaps whenever I see that tough little boat, as it was a sister ship that carried me safely through two Atlantic crossings when I knew so little about sailing that I didn't even know how little I knew. I remain shamelessly sentimental about that small fiberglass descendant of that dour Scotsman, Colin Archer.

I made myself known to an antediluvian couple puttering about on deck. The owners, a sweet, diminutive Irish lady and her time-weathered husband, invited me aboard for tea. In preparation for retirement they had bought hull and deck ten years earlier and had spent the intervening decade getting ready for some serious cruising.

The lady was curious about my experiences in the same boat and was hungry for any information about the sailorly life. She startled me with a very simple question. "What do old folk like us have most to fear?" she asked. "What are the classic errors everyone makes?"

The more I thought about that innocent question, the more I realized that there are, indeed, classic errors repeated ad infinitum and ad nausea.

It's as difficult to change human nature as it is to repeal that law of the sea declaring that sailboats are places where errors happen. Perhaps it's necessary to commit mistakes in order to learn to sail . . . something like the hazing you go through before they let you into the fraternity. I prefer to think that some thoughtful oldster, reading this, will take heed and ten minutes, thus saving trouble, money, aggravation, terror, and perhaps life itself.

I settled on ten because ten of anything seems to be just about the right number. They are here dubbed *errors*, but the term is probably not precise. Read instead *inattention to* or *carelessness* or *failure to*. These ten examples may be too personal, extracted, as they are, directly from my own blundering experience. You may know of "better" errors. I've no patent on botchery.

Here, then, are my ten classic errors. Tattoo them on the inside of your eyelids so that, even in sleep, they won't be forgotten.

I. Know Thy Boat

Sailors are endlessly willing to take a small sailing vessel on a long passage without first acquiring the drill that plays out reflexively in an emergency during which there's no time to think, only to react. An uninformed reaction can sink you, an informed one may save your life.

The best way to know your boat is to build her with your own hands, as did my antique couple with their Westsail. Then, whatever comes up (along with your dinner), you have all the needed images of how your boat is made engrained into your head, and you have the very feel of solutions to problems in your fingers. Since few of us are either so lucky or so talented or we're just too old to be able to build, the next best thing, the closest approximation, is to commission the boat yourself. You have no excuse to fail to do at least that.

Upon taking delivery of your boat, whether new or used, tear her apart as much as possible and then, piece by carefully remembered piece, put her back together again. She's no Humpty Dumpty. She'll survive the operation. She'll appreciate your hands on her rather than those of some couldn't-care-less imbecile mechanic. A commissioning is, after all, something like a honeymoon, if you can still remember that far back, and you certainly wouldn't appreciate a proxy under those circumstances.

The bilge is the part of your boat that's most vulnerable, least accessible, and most unlovely. It's the place where accidents wait to happen until a most inconvenient moment. Start from the bilge and work up. Take up the cabin sole and move in for a week.

You must understand why the mast stays up. You must become intimate with all the tubes and valves that carry fluids throughout your boat. You must have a moving picture of your steering system in your head so that when something goes wrong (as it always does) at the wrong time (as it always does), you can run the film and view the solution before you ever take wrench in hand. You must know the limits and strengths of your engine measured against the limits and strengths of your old frame. Consider the problems of fuel and filtration and of salt and sweet water and of bottom paint and of electrolysis and more. You must know your boat, its systems, its capabilities, and its weaknesses, if you're to know yourself as a serious and responsible skipper.

Unscrew everything that will unscrew, search behind all paneling and headliners, disconnect and study your marine head until you can reassemble it in the dark (you might well have to, as I did), remove all deck fittings and add the proper backup plates your builder has overlooked. Reseal them with a good, expensive sealant that a stingy commissioner wouldn't use. (Nor would he be the one dribbled upon in a cold and wet bunk.)

Take the time to stow all the spares and emergency equipment you carry so that you know exactly where they are. You may have to get to the stuff quickly when you're half underwater and your boat halfway to her beam ends.

I know of no greater or more satisfying act than to come to know the little vessel to which I'm committing my life and safety and the lives of those whom I love. Plato was once asked how man best comes to knowledge. His answer was, "Know thyself." Had he been a sailor, he would have added, "And, by all means, know thy boat."

II. Not Knowing What to Do

The first thing anyone should want to know is precisely what to do when trouble arises. The "what to do" steps for emergencies are contained in drills, of which there are only three that count for anything. Fire. Abandon ship. Man overboard.

The drills are simple and direct and must be practiced so that when an emergency arises, everyone aboard has enough information to avoid panic. Emergencies happen fast. They'll overwhelm you unless you're drilled for knee-jerk responses.

Drills are particularly important for the old sailor who doesn't move as quickly as he once did. For the old sailor it's not so necessary to act quickly as to know instantly what action to take. A reasoned, slow response to a crisis is probably the best way to act for young or old. Wild and unplanned leaping about, so typical of immaturity, is the best way to sink the vessel and kill the crew.

Fire Drill

Fire happens and kills with terrifying speed. A fire can sink your boat in five minutes. A five-minute fire drill can save both your boat and your life. All you really have to know is where the extinguishers are. It's astounding how many sailors must stop and think when asked where their extinguishers are located. An additional problem for an old head is short-term memory loss. So the older you are, the more necessary it'll be to remind yourself periodically of the absolutely basic fact of where the extinguishers are. In the one terrifying experience in which I was sprayed with burning alcohol in the galley, I went screaming on deck, absolutely forgetting the extinguisher that I'd carefully placed near the stove for just such an emergency. You can't remind yourself and your crew too many times.

It's equally astounding that most extinguishers are located where fire is most likely to happen, thus guaranteeing that they'll be in the fire and inaccessible in an emergency. Know where your extinguishers are and locate most of them far from any possible source of fire. And keep them up to date.

Abandon-Ship Drill

If the time ever comes when you must consider an abandon-ship order, you'll be exhausted, cold, wet, and terrified. If you're an old sailor, most of your reserves of energy will have been long used up in the losing battle to save your vessel. Boats are not abandoned on warm, quiet, sunny days. More likely you'll have been fighting wind and seas for hours, perhaps days, and even a young sailor might be at the end of his emotional and physical tether. That's not the moment to learn how to unlash your life raft or to wonder where the emergency rations are kept (see also pages 56 and 82 on life rafts). It's vital to think clearly, in that moment of pure anesthetizing panic, of the equipment and procedures you'll need for survival and to move slowly. Because of exigent conditions and an out-of-control boat, the emergency will preclude any quick movement. Should you not know exactly what to do and where to look, you'll be unable to rush about in a leaping, dying boat to learn what you should already have had drilled into you.

Man-Overboard Drill

Do you know the sailorly techniques needed to return to an overboard crew member from a reach or a beat or a run? Are you aware how quickly you lose sight of a person in even a moderate sea? And when you manage to sail back to your tired, scared, soggy, and perhaps unconscious crew member, do you know how to retrieve him without further injury?

The answers to these questions won't be found in any book. They'll emerge as you drill, drill, and drill for the inevitable man-overboard emergency. A young and strong crew under moderate conditions would have a 50-50 chance to recover another crew member safely. If you and your wife are an old couple, and you go overboard, there's almost no chance that your aged mate will be able to reverse course, attend to sails, steer, and keep her eye on you. You may well die in the water or even at the side of the boat when she's unable to get you aboard and still control the boat. (See page 69 for a suggestion of what to do about safety lines when a crew member goes overboard.)

Only drills can instantaneously answer all these questions and a hundred more about a crew member in the water. If you've drilled and drilled, then you're ready to go to sea. If not, then you're a fool, and the sea will find you out.

III. The Feeling Is Overpowering: Trying for Too Much Speed

The speed of a displacement hull is limited by the length of its waterline. Yet sailors, seeking speed that can't be attained, put damaging strain on their boats by carrying too much sail, and thus overpowering, in too much wind.

When you're overpowered, everything below gets tossed about, everybody gets wet and exhausted, the crew is deprived of sleep, and the boat will end up going measurably slower than it would if the rails were high and dry out of the water. If anything is going to fail, it will do so when the boat is overpowered and is already dealing with more wind than is comfortable. Not exactly the right moment to induce disaster.

Good sea sense says that when you begin to think about reefing, it's already too late. A good rule of thumb is that the longer your life has been, the shorter your sail should be. Shorten sail long before you approach the limits of control. There's a marvelous moment when, after being abused by too much wind and sea, you shorten sail and feel your boat settle down with a sigh of relief and a whispered "thank you."

IV. Looking for Trouble: Neglecting to Troubleshoot

Nylon, Dacron, stainless steel, and fiberglass require scarcely any maintenance. But even these magic materials are subject to physical deterioration not unlike what has happened to your own old muscles and bones. Lines chafe, sails break down from too much ultraviolet, and stainless can fatigue and develop mysterious cracks. Fiberglass, because of the fallible hands that lay it up, can work itself to death. Engines need oil, winches need grease, and those damned cotter pins keep falling out.

There's a three-word antidote to all this disaster about to happen. Inspect—Inspect—Inspect. An old salt I know, a sailor of as many oceans as he has decades, tells of his "morning constitutional." Upon awakening, before breakfast and before dealing with tasks clamoring for his attention, he "circumnavigates" his deck, inspecting every cotter pin, every swage, the lifelines, the lashings of deck-carried stores, and so on, from port to starboard, bow to stern. After breakfast he repeats the same exercise below. He was impressed with how many small problems, hinting at major, impending disasters, he was able to intercept.

Failure to inspect is an invitation to exigency. Use all your senses. Learn what everything should feel like, learn what things should look like, and learn the sounds they should properly make. Your old eyes may be a bit dim and your antique ears a bit dysfunctional, but it's unlikely you'll have lost your sense of smell, and simply knowing what things should smell like gives much warning of problems about to happen.

V. High Tech = High Trouble: Depending Too Much on High Tech

High tech is a fool's paradise. The first time I used a SatNav, I put my feet up, closed my sight reduction tables, sealed up my sextant, and watched the little green stars march across the screen. What a relief for this old sailor from the gut-wrenching struggle to get a star sight from a lurching, bucking deck.

Then my SatNav broke down. Since then I don't let one day go by at sea without a noon sight, the simplest sight to take, and a most carefully kept dead-reckoning log in spite of the fact that I now carry two GPS devices. Redundancy is the *penultimate* defense against the gremlins of technology. The *ultimate* defense is to know how to do without.

Dependence upon high-tech equipment is diminishing some of the very reasons we go to sea. The committed sailor finds a special joy in self-reliance, in taking neither aid nor assistance from anyone but self. The sea is the last place where you can still have the thrill of accepting total responsibility for your own actions. High tech, like some soulless robot, wants to take even that away from us.

I have no objection to a knotmeter so long as I know how

to use a chip log (see page 56). I have no objection to a depth-meter so long as I can cast a lead and read a chart. I certainly have no objection to GPS as long as I can shoot a reasonably good sun sight.

I do object, however, to those fools, old and young, who attempt to sail big oceans in little boats, relying on irreparable equipment. They know little of the underlying, old-fashioned, and simple techniques the high-tech stuff is designed to replace. When something goes wrong (and it always does), they find themselves in jeopardy and screaming for expensive assistance. The coast guard gives good succor . . . let's not waste it. And, anyway, in many cases the coast guard won't be available to assist you.

VI. Unhooked: Letting Your Anchor Slip

Every sailor can tell you about the time he dragged his anchor into a sleeping neighbor or onto a lee shore. Without exception, we all, at one time or another, have felt our security evaporate as our anchor bounced like a balloon along the ocean floor.

If everyone's ground tackle has failed them at some time, then it's clear that all of us are paying too little heed to getting our anchors down. It's not that sailors carry ground tackle that's too light for their craft. Usually the opposite is true. We simply fail to consider fully such boring matters as currents, tidal heights, and possible shifts in wind direction, all of which can so seriously affect a boat bobbing at the end of half a hundredweight of iron and half an inch of frangible nylon.

Worry about where you drop your anchor. Spend an extra half hour pulling and testing. Nag the hell out of it. Use your motor and your sails to try to pull it out of the ground from different directions, as surely the sea will try. Then, even an old guy can put on a mask and go into the water and look at it. Is it well hooked? Will the rode chafe? Will you be able to weigh it in the morning?

Practice anchoring. Practice dragging. Learn the pluses and the minuses of anchor types. Learn about holding ground and which ground each anchor prefers. Very small anchors have been known to hold big boats in terrifying conditions. But the opposite is also true . . . so beware.

There can't be any excuse for improper anchoring. Anchoring is the essence of good seamanship. And never, never, never cheat on scope!

VII. Red Sky in the Morning, Old Sailor Take Warning: Disregarding Weather Conditions

You could run your boat up on a reef. You could set her afire, or you could carefully lay her in the path of a supertanker. These events are unlikely, rare, and improbable and require conscious imbecility on your part. Weather, however, is neither rare nor unlikely and doesn't look to you for any assistance. The worst moments you'll ever have on cruising passages will be weather related.

If you're old, your ability to confront bad weather is on a downward slope. While the young sailor has survival reserves, yours may have sneakily waned, and when the clouds come down close to the sea and a dark line forms on your horizon, you're about to discover that you have fewer reserves to call up than you'd believed.

It's a homily that you can't do anything about the weather. But if you're able to glean the slightest hint of what the weather is likely to be, you're in a position to measurably improve the safety of your vessel.

The most immediate method of forecasting the weather is the sky. The sky screams its warnings, and all you need do is stop, look, and listen. This old skipper's watch on my boat is in the hours of dawning and of sunset. The rising sun casts an image of the shape of the coming weather, and at dusk the last glimpses of fading light hint at the changes the departing sun has prepared.

At these moments all your senses must be fully extended. Sight, smell, hearing, and touch all have their tales to tell. All is portent of what will happen. Look at and listen to what the patterns of the sea and sky are so stridently trying to tell you. Pay very close attention to your barometer, which can deliver very local intelligence in relative rather than absolute terms. Besides, a barometer functions adequately even when it's slightly out of whack.

Reinforce your own observations with the pilot charts, those impressive compendiums of means and averages. Ten thousand old seamen created these charts just for you. They give you a solid base of historical probability of what awaits you.

In addition to the sky, which doesn't get out of whack, there are sophisticated gadgets that do. A good VHF or short-wave radio receiver will plug you into weather frequencies around the globe. Alas, the weather that the radio reports on is rarely your own.

Gadgetry aside, always opt for what your venerable senses report and what the mind reflects. Even your past-their-prime senses grant some advantage over Aeolus. He'll kill you if you give him half a chance.

VIII. Chart Your Course

The coastal and ocean charts we use today were laboriously laid down by brave men taking soundings from open boats in strange and foreign waters. The information remains remarkably accurate. The sea is a paradox of ever-changing, never-changing aspects. Observations made centuries ago have an eerie, neoteric quality. Pay attention.

These products of intensive and informed human labor applied over very long periods of time are full of information. Winds, tides, currents, depths, bottom conditions, obstacles, dangers, lights, radio beacons, weather, and a thousand other pertinences are there for your taking. Yet many, many old sailors, perhaps because familiarity can breed contempt, fail to chart courses adequately, ignoring the wealth of information so readily available.

Charts are the only reality left when the reality of venerable senses becomes distorted. Having marine charts and knowing how to use them is like having a host of other old sailors who emerge from the dim past and, standing by your side, give you the benefit of their dateless experience. They watch over you, recounting to you their own ancient passages in these very seas. They whisper in your ear, "do this, don't do that, look out for this," and always, "be aware, be aware."

Listen to their voices. Slocum heard them, and you will, too, if you'll only listen. You're in very good company.

IX. The Captain Bligh Syndrome: Treating Your Crew Badly

A tired and hungry crew is an invitation to disaster. A crew that hasn't had its physical and emotional pelts stroked is a crew stretching beyond endurance. A hand who has spent his precious off-watch hours trying to sleep on a wet pillow because a leak wasn't repaired will be cranky, angry, and inept. When crew members are tired, cold, and unloved, the simplest of tasks is like walking under water.

The problem is that with age we all tend to get crotchety. We lose the patience of our middle years and often narrow our aging emotional horizons and lose sensitivity to the feelings of others. An old skipper who can't tune into the needs of his young crew invites, if not disaster, then at least much discomfort.

A responsible skipper knows that the safety of his boat depends upon the freely given cooperation of his crew. The level of cooperation that's required can't be demanded; it can only be politely requested and earned by example.

Sometimes it's the smallest things that count. I remember a young man on his maiden passage who, on his fifth trip to the leeward (or whoopsing) rail inquired plaintively, "Am I having fun yet, Skipper?" I assured him that he was. All he needed was the sense that someone was concerned. It helped.

So gently, old timer, gently, gently. For better or for worse your crew is all you have. Treat them with love, appreciation, understanding, and a good hot meal. They'll return it all, and more, in kind.

X. The Biggest Error of All

The biggest error of all is to ignore these errors that *everyone*—young and old, smart and dumb, old salt and young ape—commits. Attention to these potential errors won't, and can't, guarantee you safe passages, but they can short-circuit most catastrophes. Remember that ill luck is a commodity mostly manufactured by those upon whom it's visited.

As for those confrontations that you can't foresee . . . you must trust in Providence. For surely the universe must love sailors, since we were all made so beautiful.

The Old Doctor from Dubuque, a Morality Tale

Should the Bermuthas let you pass
Beware, my friend, of Hatteras
Anon.

A doctor from Dubuque, just turned sixty, had begun to feel a "mite peckish" (his diagnosis). He halved his practice, doubled his fees, and set out to acquire a sailboat with which to sail to Tahiti.

He was drawn to the sailboats of Annapolis as a hurricane draws winds into its eye. His wife, claiming a migraine and an unbreakable canasta date, declined to accompany him. She vaguely promised to meet him in Florida.

In Annapolis he fell afoul of a former used-car salesman who had become rich selling boats to retiring doctors from Dubuque. A boat was found, a price haggled out, and the colors of the upholstery decided upon, and so sea trials commenced.

Chesapeake Bay could hardly have been worse for searching out the weaknesses of a new boat. There were no seas to speak of, and the wind was a zephyrlike 6 knots. Instead of an independent expert aboard to assess the seaworthiness of the boat, a crew was impressed from among the staff and buddies of the salesman. A whole day was spent in determining the yacht's readiness to sail the great oceans, after which the doctor and the former used-car salesman agreed that there never had been a better handling or more soundly built boat. The doctor took possession of his craft and looked about for a crew with whom to waft seaward.

Absent his wife, the over-the-hill doctor found a pair of lightly oiled nubile members of the opposite sex. Each had the three requisites the doctor had been instructed, by longshore machos, to seek out in female crew. Could she tie a bowline, did she own a bosun's knife, and would she sleep with the skipper?

(Two out of three will usually do.) Both young ladies passed this rigorous test with flying bikinis. For his deckhands he chose two inexperienced longhairs who had the most yare beards he'd ever seen. They broke a bottle of the best bubbly over the bow and christened her *Elective Surgery* in honor of his disposable income. Then off they sailed, the innocent nubiles, the bubbleheaded coked-out beards, and the aging doctor in his untried and inadequate boat.

During the passage south in the Chesapeake the winds, in league with the lack of experience of crew and skipper, cooperated by never exceeding a kindly 15 knots. The nubiles were set to perfecting their knot tying and acquiring, in the Carolinas, hundreds of cans of She Crab Soup.

The doctor, in the midst of his dream, was feeling the physical strain. The yare beards were mostly moaning in their bunks or throwing up into their own faces over the windward rail. *Elective Surgery* went aground four times in the passage to Norfolk. This was no problem since the coast guard was only a radio call away. (The coast guard came to refer to them as the boat with "the old guy and the weird crew.")

They left Norfolk to round Hatteras and head into the Bermuda Triangle on their way toward Florida. They were never heard from again. They disappeared "without a trace."

The Bermuda Triangle is a chunk of the Atlantic Ocean bounded by a line joining Cape Hatteras, Bermuda, and Miami. From the time America was discovered, and continuing to the present day, more vessels have been lost in these waters than anywhere else in the world. The weather conditions in which they disappear seem exceeding mild, viewed from the safety of land, and usually the loss is "without a trace." A rich brew indeed for delvers into the diabolic, conspiracy buffs, and spinners of tales about silicon-based intelligences in flying saucers.

These mysterious losses without a trace precipitate a cascade of creepy scenarios. No mystery could be less knowable by the landlocked scenarists who dote on that "eerie body of water." Tales of the mystery of the triangle keep coming up like too much garlic in a Caesar salad. Considering the rich and evocative material for conjecture, it's little wonder that of all the importunate question marks of our bewildering universe, the Bermuda Triangle exceeds most others in the popular press.

The solutions are subtle and ingenious. To some it's clearly the work of the Devil, just a bit more of the regular mischief that keeps the old boy from dying of boredom. Others ring through a thousand changes the inescapable images of inter-galactic spaceships sucking up victims and vessels together.

Ship-devouring sea monsters are not as popular today as they were a hundred years ago, and only a few of us continue to believe that the boats simply fall off the edge of a flat world. The newer explanations mix the "black holes" of space with watery maelstroms. The really inventive, and really suspicious, lay blame on our own government's experiments with diabolical (small *d*) weaponry.

The real explanations are, alas, less exotic and less likely to be splashed about in the sensation-needing press. The real explanations of the disappearances are clearly rooted in probability, preparation and capability, oceanographics, and weather patterns. These four factors lead inevitably to the disappearances of vessels in the triangle without a trace. When we come to understand the circumstances in which boats sail in these waters, the vessels may continue to disappear, but so does the mystery.

Probability

Nowhere in the world are there more pleasure boats sailing about on the edge of an open sea. Between Hatteras and Florida there are more pleasure boats per square mile than in any other sea. This simple weight of numbers guarantees that there will be, numerically, more disappearances here than in other, less-trafficked areas. The immutable laws of chance direct that the more boats there are in a given area, the higher the probability for disaster.

Preparation and Capability

Nowhere in the world are there more small boats sailing about in the open sea with more unprepared and untrained dimwits behind the wheel who, recently come to the sea, know little of their boats' capabilities and even less of the vagaries of the sea. Most importantly, since a great number of them are older than their most recent bypass, they are unaware of the testing that the sea can give their physical capacities. The crews these old guys acquire are very nautical-appearing chaps indeed, but generally they're too young to have had the experience that teaches lifesaving respect for the sea.

The lack of preparation of the crew is reinforced by the lack of capabilities of the boats they sail. Most of the boats sold to innocents, no matter how old they are, are built in a climate of fierce cost cutting and price cutting, where expensive construction techniques, which do not show on the surface, can bury a boatbuilder under the flood of flimsy bleach bottles that his competition churns out. While some of these boats should perhaps never be untied from their docks, all are enthusiastically sold as capable of tough ocean passages. (Consider the dilemma of a broker trying to peddle a boat that he says isn't capable.) Sooner or later, these badly thought-out and lightly stuck-together cockleshells find themselves rounding Hatteras. The probability for disaster is now exponentially compounded by the lack of preparation of sailors and the incapacity of the ships they sail.

Oceanographics

Consider for a moment the geography of the Bermuda Triangle. Running up through its center is the most treacherous river in the world, the Gulf Stream. The stream whips northward from Florida for a thousand miles before it meets its first obstacle, Cape Hatteras. As the stream churns eastward to escape the jut of the cape, it runs smack into the weather patterns coming down from the North Atlantic. The hot air from the south mixes explosively with the cold air from the north immediately off Hatteras. Fast burgeoning storms are the natural result of this mixing. When the weather wants to be capricious, and around Hatteras that is all the time, the wind roars down from the north against the flow of the stream and heaps up seas of unimaginably destructive powers over shallow nearshore waters.

Everyone, let alone antique and untrained amateurs in unprepared and inadequate boats, must beware of the Bermuda Triangle.

Weather Patterns

One factor, unique to the triangle, guarantees that boats that are lost there will be lost, evocatively, "without a trace." In most cruising waters of the world there's a close downwind shore, or at least a jumble of islands, upon which an unlucky (lucky?) sailor will be blown by the prevailing winds. There's no such convenient safety net spread for the Bermuda Triangle. The prevailing wind pattern blows from the west. Toward the direction that it blows there's no land for 3,000 miles, and a sailor in trouble, or the remains of a shipwreck, are very likely to remain unsighted. Disappearance without a trace is no surprise in these waters.

Now back to the old doctor from Dubuque. Here's what happened. *Elective Surgery* sailed south from Norfolk on a lovely, bright, and sunny morning. Just one day out, when they were still close off Hatteras and still in shallow, and therefore treacherous, waters, a cold wind came out of the empty ocean to the northeast and jerked the Gulf Stream into steep and killing seas. Unable to sail back northward against seas and wind, and too inexperienced to go east to get the hell out of the stream and into deeper and calmer waters, they continued to run south. Eventually an inadequately battened-down battery came loose, spilling acid over the engine. The jenny track, which had been screwed down (not through-bolted as it should have been), tore out, allowing the jenny to whip itself to shreds. The engine was now too corrosive to touch and wouldn't start anyway on inadequate and uncharged backup batteries. The mainsail wasn't reefed until conditions were so furious that the topping lift caught itself on a spreader and ripped out a shroud. The mast, left unsupported, was tumbled down by the next nasty sea. One of the nubiles was brained in the process, and the other was thrown into the water where, because they had no man-overboard drill or experience, she quickly disappeared. It was at this moment that the good doctor went from feeling "a bit peckish" into a heart attack from which he died because neither of the yare beards had any knowledge of CPR. Then, instead of staying with the boat as long as possible, both yares were drowned while trying to launch a life raft into steep seas, a process for which they hadn't been trained.

The boat, left on its own, sailed eastward and mastless into an empty ocean. If the abandoning crew hadn't failed to close the companionway hatch, *Elective Surgery* might well have made it to Europe. She finally sank on a quiet, sunny afternoon in the middle of the empty North Atlantic without a trace.

This is a morality tale for old sailors, especially those new to the sea. Problems rarely appear singly, and as they multiply, one derived from the previous, they overwhelm the precarious reserves of age. Ancient Mariners operate on the thin edge of survival even on land, and at sea, where forces can't be matched by even the youngest and strongest, we must learn to survive by using our heads and not our antiquated frames. Preparation and drill are the watchwords. It's amazing that even among old experienced salts, there are few who can recall the last time they did an organized fire drill (see discussion of fire drills on page 189).

The old doctor from Dubuque might well have saved his crew, his own life, and his vessel by simply heeding the first law of survival at sea. Never, never overpower your boat. When you try, as did the doctor, to go where he wanted rather than where she wanted, she simply broke apart. All sailboats, even inadequate ones, are designed to accommodate to the sea, not to challenge it. Old guys like ourselves have already learned from life that survival on land and in business often is simply a matter of backing off (not backing down) and avoiding being overpowered.

All that the old doctor needed to do was to turn right, take the winds over his port, and reach the hell out into deeper and safer waters.

This is the central lesson that those blessed with many decades must take to the sea. Listen to your vessel. Go where she wants, not where you want.

Prepare and Protect

In a foreign Sea
Beset
By haters of America,
We proudly flew Old Glory.

Our pride was tested
As shots tore through
The field of blue.

Discretion, the better part of valor,
(And remembering a favorite Toast)
We ran up the ensign of
The Confederacy.

Confounded by the strange device,
Our enemies backed off.

What was the Toast you ask?
"Confusion to our enemies!"

Using the Philippine island of Mindanao as a center, draw a circle with a radius of 1,000 miles. This is the Piratic Circle. Within this circle are contained most of the world's pirates. Pirates can also be found close to home in Caribbean waters as well as within the United States' 12-mile limit. Piratical attacks on small vessels around the world are mostly carried out by fishermen blinded by the perceived "wealth" of even the poorest and most ill-found sailing vessel. Most pirates are amateurs and are likely to be lightly armed, easy to intimidate, and less than efficient in their attack.

To put matters in perspective, the probability of losing your boat in a storm is small, as is the probability of a man overboard or a fire at sea. Yet for these rare events, but not for piracy, there are carefully thought-out emergency drills, and when occasions arise, they save lives. Since you must be prepared for even the most unlikely occurrences, here are some thoughts on the who, when, where, and how of a pirate attack.

Here is what you may expect.

1. The attacking vessel will be a small native fishing boat, homemade, and outboard-powered. Long and narrow, it will be faster than any cruising monohull.

2. The attackers will usually be armed with machetes, in a very few cases with handguns or shotguns, and almost never with automatic rifles.

3. You're as likely to be attacked under way as at anchor.

4. Most attacks occur at dusk or in the early evening hours.

5. Attacks are generally mounted at your stern.

6. The similarity between a fishing boat bent on piracy and harmless boats in the vicinity will make early identification difficult.

7. Attackers always depend on stealth and surprise.

The central strategy in dealing with a pirate attack is to keep the attackers at a distance from your boat and, at all costs, *off* your boat. In order to accomplish this you must be able to identify a potential foe long before he's in grappling distance.

Early detection is the most effective weapon in your arsenal. If you can spot a piratically bent boat early enough, chances are good that the use of damaging force can be avoided. Pirates will never approach an obviously armed and alerted small vessel. The *appearance* of force, in the early stages, is as effective as the *use* of force. If you demonstrate both ability and determination to resist, most attacks will end before they begin.

Small vessels must mount a careful watch by day and by night, both under way and at anchor. Pirates will spend much time casing their prey. They make frequent and uncharacteristic passes, seeking evidence of firearms and preparedness. They'll show no lights, which is your first clear indication that there may be trouble.

There should always be two people on watch. If one watchkeeper is a woman, she should be dressed as a man. Women in the Third World, not unlike their sisters seeking auto repairs in the United States, are considered easy prey.

Since an attack is more likely to come across your stern, the watch should be mounted facing both fore and aft. The best location, especially if there's only one watchkeeper, is in the companionway facing aft. At this location the watch should have at hand lights, switches, firearms, weaponry, and other equipment positioned just inside the companionway hatch.

Your first response should be nonviolent but highly intimidating. Nothing is more effective at night than a blast of extremely bright light, especially since your attacker is hiding behind a veil of darkness. Bright lights call unwelcome attention to the attackers, blind them, give notice that the stealth part of the game is up, and serve to mask your own defensive preparations. Light is your most effective first move. Loud and abusive noise is your second. A loud hailer is good; a siren or a whooper, with its official overtones, is better.

If the pirates press on in the face of this kind of response, then be warned that they're very serious fellows and mean you harm. Most would have turned tail and sought quieter prey.

Since your decision to use lethal force is your last, and irreversible, option, it must be used when no other method will keep attackers off your boat. If you feel you have time, a few warning shots close over their heads can be effective. A firefight doesn't proceed by Marquise of Queensbury rules. You're trying to save your own life, perhaps at the expense of theirs— a messy business, but if matters have progressed this far, probably a necessary one.

Don't worry about conserving ammunition since these matters are settled very quickly. Don't worry about accuracy of fire since, in fighting off fishermen-turned-pirates, the volume of firepower is just as effective as is accuracy. Perhaps more so.

Never depend on knives or machetes as weapons of defense since your attackers will be infinitely more adept at their use than you are and would welcome the opportunity to give you a knife lesson. The whole purpose of this drill is to see to it that, whatever happens, the pirates are kept off your deck.

There are three choices among firearms: shotguns, rifles, and handguns. Shotguns are your best weapon. They're loud, require little training for effective accuracy, and, at a distance, aren't necessarily lethal. At short range, when you're in deep trouble, shotguns are invariably lethal and tremendously intimidating. A brave desperado may very well take his chances against a handgun but never against a shotgun.

The ideal defense for a small boat in home or foreign waters is a 20-gauge, pump, short-barreled, stainless steel shotgun. Pumps carry five shells, with none dangerously in the chamber. A shell can be chambered in a fraction of a second, and pumps rarely jam. For use outside of the United States they can be altered to store seven shells, and the barrel can be cut to a very short length for use in the cramped spaces of a small boat. Be aware that the legal limit for the length of a shotgun within the United States is 27 inches overall, and it may not store more than five shells. On the high seas there's no legal requirement. Shell load should never be lighter than buckshot. You can avoid shooting at people if you use solid lead slugs, which will put large holes in small boats and keep your attackers busy with inrushing water.

Always remember that the prime purpose of using firearms is to keep marauders off your boat, not to kill them. Shotguns, at the ranges at which you're likely to be using them, are loud and cheap, require little experience to use, and intimidate attackers.

Rifles are designed for accuracy and distance, neither of which is important in defending a small boat against the typical pirate attack. If you choose to carry a rifle, the best is the Russian AK47 or its superior Israeli copy, the Galil. The profiles of both are known and feared throughout Southeast Asia. An assault rifle is a devastating psychological weapon even before the trigger is pulled.

In close quarters, a handgun combines the accuracy of a rifle with the stopping power of a shotgun. In the absence of a shotgun, a handgun is the next best thing when unwelcome folk actually step on your deck. It's not quite as fearsome as a shotgun, but things can get pretty intimate on a small boat, and a shotgun needs a little room to swing in.

Avoid automatic handguns. They're a mystery to the uninitiated. Your best bet is the familiar, ever-ready, safe and simple, stainless steel six-shot revolver. It can be safely kept loaded, its rounds are visible, it's easy to reload, and in stainless steel it requires no maintenance. The proper caliber is 38. Less than that won't always stop an attacker, and more than that is unnecessary.

"Abusive exotica" is a name for those strange and unlikely devices that, either by design or by coincidence, can be made to function as weapons. The most interesting devices weren't designed as weapons. The list is limited only by your imagination and creativity, since almost anything, from a bucket of boiling water to a fire extinguisher to a quick jibe, can clear your deck of unwanted visitors.

The best of all, far better even than any gun, is the ubiquitous parachute flare. Since it's a required safety device and isn't identifiable as a weapon, you won't be hassled by its presence on your boat by the most paranoid of police. Like Poe's purloined letter, parachute flares are invisible.

Since flares are clearly not thought of as weapons, it would be hard to hold you responsible in the not-unlikely event that you mistake the local constabulary for a passel of pirates (the difference involving, in some cases, merely the changing of hats). If you shoot off a real gun at what turns out to be an official vessel, there's no way to "oops" out of it. If you should send off a flare, you might get by with "Well, it was night, and I was trying to see better, and the damned flare got out of control. I'm terribly sorry. How about a case of beer?"

Parachute flares have a substantial rocket charge designed to carry a heavy payload hundreds of yards straight up. If directed horizontally, these devices can be aimed and have a flat trajectory for a hundred feet or so. In addition to the propulsion charge, the flare is packed with yards and yards of flammable nylon and a fearsome lump of unquenchable magnesium. If one set out to build the hottest and most un-put-out-able device (short of an atomic pile), it would end up looking like a parachute flare.

A well-aimed flare will keep an attack-minded boat very busy indeed. Simply level the flare at the approaching vessel, let it fly in the general direction of the pilothouse, and the burning mess of nylon and magnesium will do the rest. In addition to the havoc it instantly creates, it also serves to light up the pirates' boat while leaving you in darkness.

I recognize the ethical dilemma that falls between the horns of unduly alarming folk who are sailing in perfectly safe waters and insufficiently preparing those who may be sailing into harm's way. The only reasonable and responsible approach to this is to fully inform sailors of where, when, and how they might face pirates, and let each devise a drill that will almost always abort an attack. The cruising fraternity has always claimed that, given the information, the individual sailor knows best his limits and his needs.

Keep in mind that your pirates are probably amateurs and lightly armed, and they'll probably run at the first sign of resistance. Keep a careful watch, keep strange boats away from your rails, and wave a "big stick" menacingly.

You'll be OK. We were.

Especially for Ancients

Doddering old folk such as we are seen as easy prey by those who would rather steal our pelf than work for a living. The problem for a criminal intent on robbing the elderly is that we rarely have much in the way of valuables on our persons.

However, if you're an old sailor and have a capable boat, you're suspected of having great wealth aboard even if it's only in the form of salable equipment or even of the sale of the boat itself.

Forays onto vessels ending in disaster and death happen close to home waters as well as along foreign shores and are too numerous to ignore. Vessels manned by old skippers are the softest targets. You must guard yourself in the event that the worst happens.

The best legal weapon for us elders is the 20-gauge shotgun previously described. It delivers a softer kick to ancient shoulders and is a powerful dissuader for unwelcome guests trying to come aboard. The 20-gauge shotgun in the confines of a sailboat is as effective as a 12-gauge, is easy to handle, and won't always mortally penetrate your assailant or blow a hole in your hull. Very little in the way of personal armament is as scary as a shotgun. It's the nuke of personal weaponry.

Unfortunately, there are as many folk along our own shores as abroad who view you as a marshmallow awaiting toasting and who view your vessel as a dollar sign. The same is perhaps as true of the near-shore harbors of the Caribbean where it's sometimes difficult to differentiate between robbers and the police.

Now that you're in your second childhood, remember your Boy Scout days and . . . *be prepared.*

So-Low Sailing

Actually it's about as low as you can get.

Young or old, being alone on a sailboat en route is a very special sort of arrogance. Only folk with a finely tuned death wish will undertake even the most miniscule sort of passage alone, including moving your boat a mere couple of berths within your own marina.

The astonishing fact is that so many sailors, especially cranky old sailors, do it, love it, and wouldn't have it any other way. Even more stupefying is that so many actually return undrowned, when common sense suggests that none should return at all.

The litany of confrontations that the solo sailor, especially an over-the-hill sailor, can face would fill this book. Any condition that can occur on a sailboat under way (or even tied up in the harbor) takes on doomsday qualities when there's no one to lend a hand. The smallest event—a sprained wrist, a wrenched back, lost glasses—and other minor irritations on land can literally kill you if you're alone at sea. Two old crocks, as a sailor friend used to say, are better than one.

What about larger matters? A broken limb, a wound, a heart attack, a tricky appendix, a crack on an ancient noggin. Any of these matters can spoil your chances of uniting again with the grandchildren.

These dolorous events happen every day to sailors young and old, but the absolute worst scenario is when *anything* bad happens to an old guy.

At sixty we're more brittle, less flexible, and more likely to take longer to recuperate from an abuse that a young chap might well shrug off. We're at risk just because we're old. We may complain that it's not fair, but we've already been well treated by the fates in being allowed to live long enough to have some trivial conjuncture threaten what's left of our lives. A small irony, perhaps, is that if we hadn't lived so long we wouldn't be so profoundly at risk. It is, however, an irony that

I choose to ignore. I eagerly trade, and don't you also, this increasing fragility for the extra decades of life granted.

Stop complaining, old friend, you have the better of the deal.

In spite of all the above, I'll confess that I understand that clan to whom harm's way seems to be a great place to be. (Why else would anyone ever ride a motorcycle?) To members of that clan, diminishing as they do daily, I concede that their need to protect their right to choose (even unto death) is more important than continuing to enjoy the company of progeny. Among this not inconsiderable group are clots of old sailors as intent on doing themselves in as they are in derring-do.

But conflicting with their need to be free is the problem of the danger that solo sailors are to others. Not only will their demise be painful to lovers and friends, but since all sailors, young and old, need sleep sometime, it's not unlikely—nay, it's common—that a sailboat with a helmsman who has nodded off can become a slow-moving but deadly projectile that will, inevitably, seek out a soft body in the water or an equally fragile hull as targets.

And if you should drop off in a more permanent sleep, or even simply drop overboard, someone at home is going to raise a big fuss that will send the coast guard on another fool's errand. They seldom have the luck of finding something when they're on a search. The odds are simply too great, and the sea is too broad. The costs in operating planes and ships for this feckless pursuit of one small body, probably already in the bellies of any number of beasts, is staggering.

So add it all up, Mr. Lonesome, damage to yourself, damage to others, agony of loved ones, and finally millions of dollars in wasted fuel and coast guard man hours . . . is this all really worth the conceit of stubbornly and petulantly wanting to do it alone?

But the best, the very best reason for you not to sail alone is that if you do, the chances are better than 6 to 5 that you'll drown your dog.

And in Defense of Foolishness

Having roundly condemned solo sailing and, by association, solo sailors, I realize that there must be some urgent push that forces folk to go alone to the sea. One such fellow, both a fit and a misfit to the arguments in this book, is David Clark, whom we first met on page 7. While I don't praise his remarkable feat and while I urge other old sailors not to replicate it, I stand in open-mouthed awe of David Clark.

When David was seventy-five, he found a rusty and aban-doned hull of a sailboat. To him it was the vessel of his dreams, and against all logic, he conceived the outrageous conceit that he would, alone, sail around the world. A solo circumnavigation is not to be taken lightly, but, one suspects, if David had given this project any serious thought, he would never have landed in Fort Lauderdale in 1999, two years and 30,000 miles of lonely sea later.

The difficulties and the trials of solo passages have been suffered by legions of sailors before Clark . . . even by some as old or older than he. The report of where he went and how he got there is not half so fascinating as the ballsy process by which he declared to his bemused family one morning that he would asailing go . . . asailing around the world yet. Asailing alone.

Looking into another's mind to get a "why" answered is a mysterious business. In a young mind, uncluttered by too much experience and unsalted by good sense, the answers to "why" are pretty easy to get. Young men do things because they can, and because young women titer up when they do.

The route into an old man's mind, hung about with hard-earned do's and don'ts and festooned with images of past tra-vails, should be an even simpler process of discovery than for a youth. While young men are unaware of the dangers they face, an old mind has all that experience to keep him safe and dry.

It should seem that way . . . and yet the evidence points south when, you would think, it should point north. Old guys (and gals), who should know better, toss the rest of their lives into a hopper, jump out of airplanes, start May-to-December romances, or, if they love the sea, often push off in a rusty and inadequate scow and, like David Clark, who knew damn all about serious ocean sailing, twinkle merrily around the world with an insouciance that belies logic.

In David's case we have a hint or two of why he did it. Not that the answers he gives reflect age-accumulated experience, knowledge, or even good common sense. No, David's answers are pure soap opera, cotton wool, romantic.

"Give it a shot. Give it a try."

"Anybody can do anything they make up their minds to do."

And, the fuzziest, most foolish, and least rational conviction that bangs helter-skelter around that old brain of his: "Dreams," he declares, "are achievable!"

If I owned a big block of stock in a corporation, I sure as hell wouldn't want David as the CEO . . .

But . . . as a sailing companion, I sure as hell can't think of anybody else I'd rather have.

So to us old coots who all of our lives strove to avoid acting foolish only in the end to discover that the striving was mostly for naught . . . I pass along David's foolish advice.

"What the hell, give it a shot!"

Against the Wind

"A Gentleman never sails against the wind."

Whether the good Cornelius "Commodore" Vanderbilt was quoted correctly or whether the exhortation to never sail against the wind is entirely apocryphal, it remains good advice, especially for those of us for whom this book is written. Sailing against the wind is like trying to fly in the face of logic. It's unnatural, uncomfortable, and unproductive. It's an activity best performed by loutish youths who compose the crews of racing boats. Sailing against the wind is showy and vulgar. If you have the good taste and the good breeding not to wear argyle sox with a tuxedo (or perhaps anytime), then why in the world would old you want to sail against the wind?

It is, of course, quite possible to sail against the wind. In fact, your boat is perversely designed to accomplish just that direction, although with great strain to rigging and crew. In spite of the fact that most sailing is accomplished off the wind, designers still are judged by how close to the wind their latest hulls and rigging can cling, no matter with what discomfort. This is like measuring the worth of an ancient physique by the single measure of how much iron he can pump. Old bodies aren't meant to pump iron, old sailors aren't meant to sail against the wind, and, I suspect, inching a degree ever closer to Boreas is much like that feckless, heartbreaking, and dangerous search for the Golden Grail. Why bother?

I'm convinced that most cruising sailors will lay a course into the wind only as a last resort or, if they've not yet reached an age of some wisdom, to demonstrate their bravery to an attractively rounded crew member. The last time I tried to sail into the wind was on a passage from Sri Lanka toward the Maldives at the wrong time of the year. I use the word *toward* advisedly, since we never did complete that particular passage. After six days of beating the bejesus out of our boat, our patience, and our love for our fellow man, I glanced back longingly in the direction of the harbor we had left days before and watched, to my horror, as it hove again above the horizon. After six days of accepting cold salt water in the face and bearing the abuse of body and spirit, I said to hell with it, declared that discretion was the better part of valor, turned tail, and ran back to Sri Lanka. The sail back took six hours and was wonderful.

There's a special kind of rapture associated with sailing with the wind. It's a curious reprise of youth. Everything is soft, easy, and nonthreatening. Just as you'd always hoped that your increasing decades would be. As you come off the wind, it suddenly becomes your friend, and the seas, which a moment before were trying to beat your brains out, now fawn with an eager desire to help you along. Your boat, which on any close point of sail is forced to strain and labor and to go in directions that it simply doesn't wish to go, lopes gaily along. Hull and sails accept the urging, rather than the demands, of a softer wind and a gentler sea. Isn't it more sensible to be pushed than to be vectored?

On the wind old bones feel warm, since the wind is now from the back and is diminished exactly by the speed of boat progress with it. A wind at the back is always less enervating than one blowing into one's face. Eyelids and facial muscles relax, and grimaces of tension, born of the winds of affront, are gently massaged away by the zephyrs astern. You've made magic. You've tamed Boreas. You've taken the wind out of your sails, in the ancient language of the sea. You recall with pleasurable superiority Commodore Vanderbilt's edict and giggle at the transformation of wind to whisper and you from stumblebum (which was always your opinion of yourself) to gentleman.

And all at no cost, other than the slight bother that you may not be going precisely (or even approximately) toward your intended landfall. At your age, do you really have to get somewhere right away? Won't anywhere, any old time, do? But hold! Is it really all that easy? Are there no negatives? None? Is the physics of life that's taught you (the hard way) that payment is extracted for pleasure suddenly reversed, declared null and void?

Alas, the piper, which you had hoped to be Piper-Heidesieck, still has to be paid. The physics has held, and you slowly discover, as the memory of the agony of beating into the wind fades from your mind, the price of the bargain you've made with the wind. If Faust had been a sailor, the Devil would've offered a run downwind instead of eternal life.

Running (sailing downwind) has inherent in it three seeds of sudden misfortune, any one of which can lead to loss of life or boat or both. The threat is more acute because the action of running has the appearance of safety. The sailor is lulled, his awareness blunted, his defenses down.

Here's a worst-case scenario. You're coasting downwind in about 12 knots of wind. Since your forward speed is about 7 knots, you seem to be flying through a proximate calm. What can possibly happen? Well, how about this? The wind picks up from 12 to about 20 knots, but to you it still is apparently only 13 knots caressing your back, still a gentle breeze. As the wind freshens, as it's wont to do, it backs a bit to starboard, and the stronger breeze increases the roll, which sailboats love to do downwind. You now have 20 knots of dangerously disguised wind, your main boomed out to starboard, and a wind direction that's moved, unsuspected, in that direction, toward your leech (the free-swinging end of your main). As your boat rolls a little more to port in response to the stronger breeze, the more starboard wind catches your main in an uncontrolled jibe, sweeps your deck clean of two or three crew members, snaps your mast, rips out your port shrouds, and leaves you helpless, mastless, sailless, unable to get back to pick up the crew overboard, some of whom may very well have been killed by the boom or knocked senseless and drowned.

You try to start your engine and find that the halyards, sheets, and shrouds trailing about you in the sea have fouled your propeller, and you now realize that the freshening breeze has turned into a dangerous squall. You're about to pay the piper. If you think this scenario is far-fetched, just ask any salty old blue-water sailor what his recurrent, most terrible nightmare is.

While an uncontrolled and unsuspected jibe is the most dramatic threat of downwind sailing, there's a threat more pervasive, as expensive, and, ultimately, as dangerous to a boat far at sea.

Chafe!

For every point of sail except for running, the chafe problem, the bane of babies and sailing ships, has been brought under control. In beating and in reaching, a little attention to chafe will protect your precious sails and lines. In running, the wind and the designers, to the greedy applause of the sailmakers, conspire to destroy sails in an hour that are expected to last for years. And if you're far at sea (and there's nowhere else worth being), and if you have no spare main (and how many of us do?), then the piper calls again.

The odd thing is that it's easy to deal with these disasters waiting to happen to you. As terrible as are the consequences of chafe and lulling and the uncontrolled jibe, it's just so simple to avoid them.

Chafe happens mainly to your main. It can be plainly seen that the shrouds and the spreaders are the chief enemies of your sail fabric, as they both provide available hard surfaces upon which to rub. Since your staysail and jennys are forward of these devils, you must seek to protect your main. It's astounding that so serious a problem with so obvious an answer is so seldomly addressed.

To avoid chafe downwind, never, never, never sail with an unreefed main. Take two deep reefs, even in mild weather, and the head of your main comes down below your spreaders and comfortably aft of the shrouds. You lose remarkably little speed since sail area is less critical and less elastic a factor downwind than it is either beating or reaching. And as a bonus, if you should jibe, the power and the speed of a boom with a reefed main are substantially reduced.

To avoid a jibe, always, always, always secure a line from the end of your boom to a good heavy cleat at your bow. Such a line is called a preventer. It's designed to prevent you from killing yourself. Next question.

To avoid being lulled. Well now, that's not so simple. The lulling happens because the following wind is diminished by the forward speed of the boat. Try wearing about a couple of times from a quiet run into the wind and sense, as you will with shock, the power that's hanging over your creaky old shoulder. When running, pay closest attention to the slightest change in either wind direction or velocity. Changes kill. At sea, as in life, an unaltered state is rarely dangerous; an altered state always is—as we learn in the process of changing from a young to an old animal.

Humans are a forward-looking species. Our ears point forward, our eyes point forward, and our noses hang out ahead of everything, forever sniffing out what lies foremost. And we're always getting killed, incredibly surprised, by a stab in the back. We never do learn that aft lies our unprotected backsides. So when a wind comes from your rear, full of pillow talk and soft promises, you can be damned sure that you're about to receive a whack on the ass.

In describing his ideal woman, a libidinous artist yearned for a lady with three breasts, two in front and one in the back. "Marvelous to dance with!"

A downwind sailor needs "one in the back," too. Something a bit more sensory than, if not so attractive as, a bosom. Perhaps an old sailor's wary and suspicious eye.

Storm Management

Dealing with storms and high winds for an old sailor is altogether a different matter than for a passel of deck apes who view storms as a challenge to their manhood. Old sailors have less to prove about themselves and have fewer resources available to waste on dealing with a storm.

The trick is never, never fight a storm. Accept defeat even before the winds come down on you. Bend and accommodate like the ancient and limber willow that you are.

Storms come in three flavors, all of which have different characteristics, but all of which we should deal with in exactly the same manner.

There are quick-building squalls, slow-building high winds of gale force, and, heaven forbid, hurricanes and typhoons. There are shelves full of books that advise what to do in an unavoidable storm. But for old sailors whose energies are limited and whose threshold for caution should be higher than that of the young, there are only three rules that will deal with any storm situation.

Rule 1 is to choose not to sail where and when storms are. It sounds simple, but the truth is that this is the best advice that we can ever follow. Never sail in hurricane season, June through November, in the vicinity of the fourteenth parallel, and avoid sailing in the North Atlantic from August to May. These are the times when your boat can be tested to destruction. These are the times when you might find that crises of wind and seas, which you were capable of handling a few decades back, are now beyond your abilities. Discretion being the better part of valor, choose to sail when the sea isn't intent on killing you.

Rule 2, applicable to both squalls and gales, is to shorten sail at the first hint that something is coming your way. Again, discretion being the better part of valor, it's infinitely better for an old sailor to get his canvas in and then find that he didn't need to do so than to wait too long and find himself in trouble.

Young crew members, who can handle sail changes in high winds, can properly wait it out to see if the threat is momentary. Old sailors don't have that luxury. The older you are, the earlier you should be shortening sail.

Since I don't like furling devices for serious sailing, the quickest way to get a hanked jib down is with a downhaul led back to the cockpit. Downhauls also work with mains, but it's much safer, in all but the highest winds, to maintain control of your vessel with some canvas aloft. Reefing should always be done at the mast, my old and slightly creaky friend, so give yourself plenty of time. Better to act quickly and be thought of as a fool than to wait too long and be proven a fool.

Rule 3 is for when you're in extreme winds and seas. These can be a building gale that will exhaust you before it sinks you or a hurricane that will exhaust your old energies at about the same time that it sinks you. Rule 3 is your final acknowledgment that the sea is your master and that to survive it you must give in to it.

Rule 3 is to lie ahull. Except in those rare cases when you've foolishly allowed yourself to come too close to land, lying ahull, like a magic wand, takes the debilitating pressure off you and your vessel. Winds that felt like the furious end of the world while you were still fighting a storm now become, in comparison, almost halcyon.

To lie ahull, all you need to do is strike and tie down all sail, secure your rudder amidships, and clear the deck of stuff that might blow away. Then go below, batten down all hatches, and take to your bunk. You'll find the a vessel ahull has a soft and easy motion since it's bobbing about, corklike, and offers no opposition to seas and winds. As a bonus, now that you're safely cocooned below, the shattering and dismaying roar of high winds are a distant murmur.

We were sailing north from Milos toward Athens in the Aegean, a most unpalatable and disagreeable sea in spite of what the Greek Tourist Board claims, when we ran into a nasty little storm. The typical square waves of the Aegean arose, and we couldn't make good to windward. The more we tried to control the boat, the more unruly she became, much like a willful child when pushed to act against its wishes.

We'd tried reefing, heaving-to, trailing warps, and all of the other tactics of control we knew. Finally we realized the *Unlikely* was asking to be decontrolled, to be allowed to do what she knew best, to survive. "Go below," she seemed to say, "and leave this bit of nastiness to me." And so we did. Sails down and furled, engine off, tiller tied amidships, we gratefully went below, sealed the boat against noise and water, tucked ourselves tightly into our bunks, had a glass of wine, and left *Unlikely* alone. Lying ahull simply means getting out of your boat's face. Nine hours later, *Unlikely* bobbed up out of the subsiding storm, with no damage and infinitely less strain on the boat than when we were pressing her to do what we wanted rather than what she wanted. In those nine hours, as we comforted ourselves below, *Unlikely* had simply bobbed about like a cork and drifted a bit to lee. When we measured her drift, which could be a problem on a lee shore, we found that she had made only 3 miles to lee.

Rule 3 saved our lives, our energies, and our good humor. Especially our good humor.

Entrance

When I was fifty and feeling young and foolish, I flew seven hundred friends to Paris for a weekend birthday bash. The high point of the weekend was a formal ball held in one of the Rothschilds' palaces.

At the time I was gaga over a lady who, as only ladies can, changed my life. She was stunning, rich, passionate, and what was more important for this old sailor, she knew how to make an entrance.

Her entrance at the fancy dress ball was memorable. Even today, thirty years later, when old friends get together someone will always ask, "Do you remember Suzy's entrance?" We all do.

She chose the perfect moment. Later than fashionable. The other guests were already in the ballroom and had the time to take the edge off with a few drinks. Suzy left nothing to chance.

The normal entrance was through a pair of gilded portals at floor level, through which everyone had dutifully trooped. Not Suzy. She had noticed a lovely stairway descending from a balcony at the other end of the room, and she contrived to have the secret and private doors to the balcony unlocked for her.

At the proper moment she appeared quietly, without fanfare, at the top of the steps. She wore a simple, skintight white silk gown, revealing one perfect, naked shoulder. A white headband bound her dark hair to her head. She made every other woman in the room feel mildly inadequate, but as she was such a great lady as well as a great beauty, their feelings lacked jealousy.

She waited quietly at the top of the stairs, at complete ease. First one, then another, then, slowly, all in the room lifted their eyes to her. The room quieted. Still she waited, interminably, till it seemed that the scene would freeze forever like a diorama. Finally, she slowly extended one perfect, bare foot and descended the first step. The room, holding its breath till then, let out a sigh of relief and anticipation.

The rest was history. She owned the night, the room, and my heart.

I tell this tale because of the pleasure it gives me in the recall and because it defines a most important event in sailoring: the entrance to the harbor.

Like Suzy's entrance, your entrance to a harbor, as we shall see, must be perfectly timed, and your boat must be in consummate good order, dressed in proper flags and ensigns. The action of entering must be accomplished with unembellished exactness, with not one move unnecessary and without loud and evident direction to crew. Your boat should appear to bring herself in, just as Suzy appeared to float down the staircase, an inch or so above the steps.

The entrance to a harbor, with every eye on you, with your peers waiting to judge your every move, must be poised, polished, suave, and urbane. You must make all the other boats feel a tad inadequate . . . but without jealousy.

An entrance is preceded by a landfall, certainly the high point of any passage. To watch, after days or weeks at sea, the goal of all your efforts rise on your bows, expected and hoped for, is precisely what sailoring is all about.

Perfect landfalls follow a scenario inscribed in centuries of experience. Those old sea dogs among you who've searched a distant coastline for entrances and landmarks know how utterly mysterious the smudges along the horizon can be. Even on closer approach, entrances can be obscure, points and capes can be foreshortened, and the whole picture can be distorted by your own burning desire to make port.

There's one fail-safe way to make a landfall. Only incontestable, unerring navigation lights point the way to a safe harbor. But since you should rarely chance a night entrance, navigation lights are to be used just before dawn, in the few moments before they turn off. As dawn breaks, there's a moment of pure twilight, a moment of revelation, when navlights still point the way and shore features meld lucidly with the beckoning lights. What you see on your chart coalesces in your mind's eye with the lights and the outline of the coast ahead of you.

Always make your landfall at dawn. If you're too early to match lights to land, wait a bit. Never, never be late, because if you are, that narrow channel leading to your refuge from the sea will be unlighted and may be draped in the mists of morning or hidden in a confusion of mountains.

If you're on a sailboat, old sailors will advise that you come in under sail. It's more than just elegant. It's a prideful and satisfying statement that you know what you're doing. Coming in under sail is the safety net you spread lest your engine fails.

Engine failures happen most frequently in the harbor, after long disuse at sea. Connectors corrode and seals leak and electrics poop out in response to the leaping about at sea. Plastic bags and floating lines tempt your prop. Indeed, after weeks under sail, you yourself may lose the correct touch on the throttle that keeps your engine alive.

Keep your engine ticking over if you like, even motor sail into the harbor, but always keep your main up.

Take your time. Like Suzy, make a long and searching pause, enough for you to register all friends and foes. Seek out unexpected dangers, and give the folks at anchor time to anticipate your arrival. At dawn, nothing is worse than a surprise bump or clank of chain released too close by. Give the boats at anchor a chance to help you find the perfect spot to put your hook in.

There's nothing, no matter how old the sailor, in all your experience like that ineffable moment when, after the terrors and trials of a long sea passage, you finally feel your anchor grip in a safe and protected harbor. You feel the muscles of your neck go slack and the tensions in your head dissipate. Careful sailorly responsibility and hard labor are rewarded by an absolute sense of a task well completed.

How seldom in your life ashore have you received such perfect affirmation. Ashore, there's always something else to be done, some contingent task hanging fire. Someone, something, always seems to block that utter sense that, as in the ancient sailor's call, all's well. On land there's simply too much input, too much clutter of people, too many comings and goings, too much ferment, too much emotional "noise" to allow a total moment of respite.

Those moments of concord and tranquility are reserved for the sailor come home from the sea.

Your anchor is down, the journey is complete, and you have absolutely nothing left to do except fall happily into a bunk that isn't trying its best to toss you out. It's a state of sailorly grace. You may now drift off to sleep with the sure knowledge that you've done your duty and that when you awake, after sleeping as much as you like, you may start to plan your next passage.

Personal Observations

Rhythmns

Sailors
Measure tides,
Acknowledge night,
Watch Moon's shape,
Sun's height.
Stand watch on cosmic rotations,
And sail great oceans
In enchanted concord.

As I struggled to control a small sailboat with a large outboard, I watched a half-scale racer whip through the confused waters of the Longport entrance and slip up quietly to the dock. When I investigated I was astounded to discover a vessel sans engine and a sailor sans nothing.

—Reese

Don Cohan on Cruising and Racing

One of my life's high moments occurred when I came ashore after racing and had my seven-year-old grandson tell me that I was his hero and my nine-year-old granddaughter state that I was "the greatest." Two years earlier I had finished going through aggressive chemotherapy for the second time, with accompanying radiation. I never thought I'd race a sailboat again. I was seventy years old. After two years of not having set foot in a sailboat, I was pressured by my family to race the Atlantic Coast Soloing Championships. I won it (for the fourteenth time) in a heavy-air last race, beating a top sailor in a surfing spinnaker finish by a few feet, with my family anchored at the finish line yelling, "Go, Papa Don." What more could you ask?

I'm a schizophrenic sailor because I enjoy both cruising and racing. After converting an old 50-foot Fyfe-designed and -built 8-meter into a cruising boat, my wife and I took our honeymoon forty-two years ago. Together we've cruised from the Chesapeake to Maine, and some of the happiest times of my life have been spent messing about a boat with my wife, Trina. We've enjoyed our joint sailing adventures and the experience of being hidden away from the rest of the world in our own snug anchorages. Sailing a 50-foot boat requires two people who can do the "sea tango." We still find joy and wonder in memories of being fogbound in a fast-moving Vineyard Sound current and together working our way into Menemsha or being caught off Block Island in a blow where the genoa shredded, and it took the two of us a great deal of effort to get it under control.

Not many marriages would have survived the last day of our honeymoon. My conscientious wife insisted on being back at work as she had promised. The coast guard issued an incorrect weather report that resulted in our meeting Hurricane Brenda head-on when we tried to cross from Cuttyhunk to New Bedford (Massachusetts) in 1968. We pounded to the head of Buzzards Bay and into the Cape Cod Canal and finally fought our way into Onset and luckily picked up a secure mooring. I felt not only relieved but quite heroic, having protected my bride and come through the harrowing experience, handling a 50-foot sailboat in hurricane winds. After tying up I turned in glory to my bride, expecting my just rewards, but all I got was a cold stare and a verbal blast of "Cook your own damn dinner—you did not pay any attention to me on the last day of our honeymoon." I still like messing about in boats with her and having a summer home that enables my family to appreciate the water and have their own "sea happenings."

Back in 1967 I decided I wanted to make the U.S. Olympic Sailing Team to compete in Germany in the 1972 Olympics. After much hard work and family encouragement, I was able to do it, and I won an Olympic medal. I enjoy the self-testing and all the other facets of racing at top-level international competition. I absorb and savor the milieu and the interpersonal relationships while committing myself completely to achieve in the sport. I block out the world's chatter. I have raced in the various Olympic-class boats in the United States from north to south, east to west, Canada, Puerto Rico, the Bahamas, Italy, France, Germany, England, Australia, the Netherlands, and Sweden. In these various Olympic classes I've been Chesapeake Bay Champion, Pacific Coast Champion (twice), Atlantic Coast Champion (fifteen times), U.S. Champion, European Champion, German Champion, and Australian Champion, and I've won one of the windiest Kiel Week Regattas. What a "Jacob's coat of many colors" these happenings have been. Sociologically it has been an eye-opener to see the response of the sailors and spectators to the United States when I sail. Little can give you a better sense of how people respond to our country than to live with and compete against sailors from all over the world. Being a representative of America has always made me aware that I must act (as I hope I would, anyway) in a proper and worthy manner. No "winning at any cost." You learn a great deal about yourself when you're in a competitive pressure cooker. It's easy to be a hero when all is well, but you have to be the same person when it hurts.

I'm now seventy-two, and sailing, both cruising and competing, has been a very important part of my life. Now sailing and the sea give me another gift. I'm aware that I'm on the downwind side of the hill, and the reawakened goal of being a competitive sailor has caused me to stir up banked fires and rejuvenate neglected physical abilities. In 2002 I won the Soloing U.S. Championship and finished fifth in my fifteenth World Championship. Think of what being a competitive sailor is doing to slow down the aging process and keep the downhill side of my mountain challenging and interesting.

I have been so fortunate in my life. I include my love of the sea in all its shading as a meaningful part of my existence. How lucky I am at seventy-two to be planning more briny challenges, believing in my ability to still be competitive and to have the opportunity to test my expectations— and to still be a player. Wow!

—*Don Cohan, 2002*

Old Sailors Get It Right

It is not true
That old sailors never die.

It is true
That sailors die, like cowards, a thousand times
Each day they are not at sea.

It is true
That old sailors never die
At sea.

Each time, and it happens with depressing frequency, I see another picture of hale young human animals lolling about in an immaculate white sailboat on a quiet sea, I want to shout from the rooftops, "No, no, it's all a lie!"

These photos, endlessly perseverated, imply that cruising a sailboat is a sport for the young. When was the last time you saw a sailboat ad in which the lolling about was done by a beat-up old guy and his less than sylphlike mate? I'll tell you when. Never.

By implication, and by iteration of image in sailboat brochures and in any soap opera that might include a sailboat, old folk don't exist. Sailing is sold as a sport for young, smooth-skinned male juveniles, displaying large pectorals as progenitive encouragement for unwrinkled and upthrust female crew members.

Sag and droop has no place in the iconography of sailing. A wrinkled skin is as bad as a wrinkled luff, and any sign of aging of boat, crew, or line that can't be cured with fiberglass, face-lift, or money, bans vessel and sailor from the covers of sailing magazines.

Please note that I emphatically didn't say that racing, as a *sport* for the young, is a lie. Indeed it's one of the great truths, Don Cohan excepted, that only the young are equipped with the fortitude, femurs, and foolishness necessary for the racing of sailboats. The involvement in racing is a simple extension of sexual aggression. The winners get the girls.

Watch any young sailor in 10 knots of zephyr on a flat sea. Boredom sets in with the suddenness of a black squall and can be alleviated only by the appearance of another sailboat. No need for a challenge. Sheets get tightened, sails are trimmed, the boom is tugged inboard, and the rail approaches the sea. The young sailor, rather than savoring the pleasures of nature, is going to show the other boat (and his own lithesome lady) just what sailing (and by implication his masculine effectiveness) is all about.

The urge to race a sailboat is closely akin to the need to do battle and to the endless struggle to improve the health of the species. The true functions of the young are to die gloriously in battle and to perform energetically in bed; both are curiously connected to the blind passion to extract one-eighth of a knot more from nature than the adversary can.

In racing it's all muscle, speed, dexterity, and the ability to endure, in the presence of the sailor's ladylove, unnecessary pain for short and critical periods of time. These are the attributes of the young animal.

But while racing is for the young and crazy at heart, certainly the sailing life, bar the need to extract eighths, is the ultimate sport for those of us who've lost the youthful passion to compete and to win. We Ancient Mariners may lack some muscle, some dexterity, some eyesight, and some hearing, but in the great compensatory biological game, we've replaced them with patience, experience, and respect for nature.

The sailing life is truly a sport for the old.

The sailing life gives us old folk the opportunity to escape from the probing eyes of our children, intent, as they are, to discern in us the earliest evidence of faculty loss. Our progeny view us as an appendix soon to be disposed of, and they too closely count our remaining days while all we old folk want to do is ignore our mortality. To be in your own boat, unjudged and unmeasured, adds years not only to your life but to your enjoyment of whatever life you have left.

On the other hand, to live, like most grandpops and grandmoms, as an irrelevant relic on the inevitable downward path of life, impacted within a flock of gray-skinned, knobby-kneed, and purposeless oldies, isn't living at all. We (if you, my reader, are as old as I) must escape from the tyranny of the young and avoid relegation to retirement homes, holding tanks for the truly old and decrepit. Both are unacceptable modes of living out the last third of life.

Participation in violent physical activity does, indeed, come to an end sometime. Our bodies do have time limits that vary with the sport. A gymnast at twenty is considered a hundred years old. Football is out of the question at forty, boxing is questionable at thirty, and golf scores soar at sixty.

But there are sports, given participants have congenial genes, in which youth is not the first and last requirement. The king of the Danes played a good game of tennis at ninety, and a friend of mine is still jumping out of airplanes at sixty-five. As long as you aren't driven to winning, most sports have a long drawn-out endgame.

Let's consider debility, the loss of physical skills. What's really needed to sail a boat? What are the real endgame sailorly skills?

First is experience, that irreplaceable store of information. The sure knowledge, characteristic among old folk, that they've faced similar crises before and survived worse. Sailing experience is purely a matter of the passage of time combined with the doing of sailing. It is, for example, almost impossible to teach the reefing of a sail. That experience is etched into muscle. The etching is ineradicable, and the learning is only achieved by doing.

There are so many things that have to be done on a sailboat, and have to be done well, that time becomes the only measure of all the skills required. The doing, and the time to do, are the best definition of experience. Experience, the antonym of youth, can be acquired by the young only by growing old.

On board a vessel manned by young and energetic sailors, a crisis is met with instant response as if a tenth of a second counts. Frenetic barreling about too often results in a catapult over the lifeline or, with boring regularity, a broken bone or a deck slippery with blood.

Old folk are, thank goodness, unable to respond with high alacrity, so we are spared the sea dunk or the bone break, and our vessel is spared the need to face up to a compounded crisis. When you do things too quickly on a sailboat, one damn thing leads to another damn thing. Few single crises ever sunk a sailboat, but when the original confrontation is burdened with fast and unthoughtful activity, disaster looms. Old guys and gals are better sailors than young animals because we simply can't move fast enough to magnify disaster. Leaping up and doing for the sake of doing is a sure prescription for calamity.

A nice old guy I know once described to me his mode of dealing with crisis. "I ease the sheets, then I carefully find a course which the boat likes. Then I go below and have a small glass of wine, and I think about the problem. By this time the crisis has either cured itself, which they do without my assistance nine times out of ten, or, when I return on deck I have a clear idea of what I shall do."

This fits into my conviction and my experience that almost nothing on a sailboat must be done in a hurry. Speed in response to crisis is best replaced by careful preparation for potentially dangerous contingencies. Thus we're back to experience. Since it takes a long time for all the bad things that can happen to a sailor to happen, a great sailor must, perforce, be an old sailor.

Harelike leaping about is demonstrably more dangerous than a tortoiselike crawl. The devilment that a sailboat can do to you appears slowly, with great dignity and gentlemanly forewarning. Your response should be the same. Dignity, with which we old folk replace derring-do, is inherent in age. Dignity is the shield behind which we hide our infirmities. It's the even pacing that allows us to do stuff slowly that we can no longer do quickly.

I had been taught a lesson by Sir Humphrey Barton, the

master of the *Mary Rose* and the founding admiral of the Ocean Cruising Club: on a sailboat, less effort is preferred over more effort to accomplish a given task. When a task is accomplished with no evident effort at all, perfection has been reached. Since that day, I have ambled about my boat, keeping my head while others have been losing theirs, and murmuring thanks to the memory of Sir Humphrey. Now that I am as old as Sir Humphrey was then, I am even more grateful.

Barring fire, or an uncaring whale, there's no crisis that must be addressed quickly on a sailboat that couldn't have been avoided in the first place with forethought. Even in the case of fire, the positioning of extinguishers and some fire drills (patience, forethought, and experience) will limit damage (for more on fire drills see page 189). In the case of a whale who neither sees nor feels you, there's little to be done except to quietly step up into your life raft as your boat slips away beneath you.

Collision with another ship doesn't even enter into my lexicon of sailing. If you're so dumb, in a big ocean, to fail to mount a continuous and careful watch, then you won't live long enough to be old enough to fit my argument.

Of all of our senses, touch is the most important to a sailor, especially at night, which is a full half of sailing time. Thankfully this is the last sense to go. Taste is irrelevant, and the sense of smell stays with you a long time.

I once made a landfall in Senegal, after all my instruments went out, by following the smell of the desert down the coast of Africa until we encountered the rich and pungent smell of the city of Dakar. I simply turned left at the odor and followed my nose into the harbor.

Hearing has lost its cruciality since lowing buoys and tintinabulating bells have been replaced by radar. And anyway, the sounds that are really important to a sailor aren't those distant sounds; they're the creakings and the clangings and the swishes of the boat itself. These are vibratory sounds, more felt in the body than heard in the head.

Loss of sight is the great fear of old sailors. But sight doesn't shut down like a diesel with air in its lines. It fades slowly, and as with most biological events, there are accommodating parallels. In vision you lose acuity, but as you sailors know, it's not what you actually see at sea, but what you sense you're seeing. Long before you can pick out the two masts of a ketch on the horizon, you've already decided that what you're seeing feels like a ketch. Long before you can delineate the masts that a big ship carries and from which you can, with surety, determine its speed and heading, you'll have decided, without actually seeing the ship, whether or not you are in any danger.

The progenitive drive, at least among sailors, never does seem to go. I was tied up in Larnaca next to a lovely schooner whose home port was Hollywood. I should have been forewarned.

The crew of two Ancient Mariners were busily making ready for sea but had a moment to get friendly with my wife, who is some decades younger and considerably more beautiful than I. One of them was tall and thin with long silky hair and described himself as "seventy years old with a slight hump." The other, more Hollywood looking, had a deep, ginny, theatrical voice and was draped with some thousands of dollars worth of gold chains.

Since my wife had in tow an ancient like themselves, they must have considered her fair game. The proposal they made to her, unabashedly and within my hearing, will forever be synapsed in my mind.

"How would you like," they inquired of my lady, "to try 140 years of experience?"

My advice to the young sailor is to await with eagerness the coming of old age, in which the best of the sailing life resides.

My advice to my circle of beloved ancients is to just keep sailing. Don't let your kids tell you you're too old for adventure and new horizons. Don't let your doctor dissuade you, for while he may know much about death, what does he really know about life? Don't let society impose its "shoulds" and its "shouldn'ts." Tell your accountants and your stockbrokers that, in this best time of your life, they're simply redundant, and tell your lawyers to go to hell.

Finally, don't die on some foreign soil. Should you be so foolish, the cost of airfreighting the remains, the undertakers, the preparations, the traveling, and visits attendant on a funeral will bend your estate and give unnecessary pain to your progeny.

Not to mention the obscene cost of a casket.

Tell your undertaker to join your lawyer.

Die in passage, and let the sea be your final harbor.

An Old Sailor's Luck

Fool not with luck
My sailor friend.
Accept its gift.
Should you claim skill
Or act of will
The Sea's revenge
Is swift.

My father, of blessed memory, opined, "Success is 50 percent luck and 50 percent ignorance. All you need in life is to be dumb and lucky. Smart helps, but the important thing is to be lucky. You can't beat luck."

The flaming fuel episode in mid-Pacific would have done me in without those five large jars of Silvadene my son happened to stow on board. Anything less might have killed me. Later, when I asked my son why he chose five jars, he shrugged and said he just felt that five would be the right number.

Luck.

On my first Atlantic crossing, when at fifty I was green as a sailor, a supertanker at 25 knots came out of nowhere and cleared us by 10 feet.

Luck.

At sixty I was sailing with a following wind in the Indian Ocean when the forestay snapped. The wind, from aft, held my mast up.

Luck.

As we approached the coast of Oman in the Indian Ocean with the broken forestay, the only harbor we could make was an empty little settlement at the barren tip of that empty little country. Where were we to find someone who could weld the stainless fitting that had snapped?

In that lonely and forsaken place, at that precise moment, there was a team of English engineers with all their equipment flown down for a few days from the capital to service one of the sultan's downed helicopters. Welding stainless? "No problem, mate."

Luck.

I lost my mast in the Red Sea off the coast of what was then communist Ethiopia, the worst place in that worst of all seas to be. Instead of the mast crashing to the deck, as is usual, the spar sighed, tilted softly over, and slid gently into the sea after we cut it away with a Kalashnikov with nine lucky shots.

Luck.

My wife, Marilyn, whom I love dearly, is a great sailor.

Luck.

At eighty plus, I'm still sailing.

Luck, courtesy of the Great Genetic Lottery game.

Luck is not usually identified by nationality, but two of my best pieces of luck, having to do with people, were with Germans. One was the worst human being I ever met, and the other was the best. Both, in their own way, served me well when I needed a stroke of luck.

I was laid up in Djibouti with a broken mast. No one in Djibouti knows anything about sailing and certainly absolutely nothing about rigging a new mast to a serious 46-foot cruising sailboat. What I desperately needed was a sailor, good with tools, knowledgeable about rigging, and, because facilities were at a minimum, immensely strong.

Our new 70-foot mast arrived from France one morning while we pondered our dilemma and rued our fate. There was no way that I could handle the job, and I would certainly not let a Djiboutian near my boat.

At that moment a nice 36-footer sailed into port. No sooner had the hook been set when I watched a huge blond bear lift a hard dinghy overboard with one hand and row swiftly to my boat.

It was Ziggy, 6 feet, 3 inches, all muscle, thirty-six years old, and, as I learned later, a master rigger since he'd had to build and rig his own boat to escape from the Spanish equivalent of Devil's Island, where he'd been confined for killing one (or two, I never got that straight) mates in the Spanish Foreign Legion. Ziggy had defected to the Spanish Legion from Germany, having been involved in other serious peccadilloes.

Ziggy, a devil in a sailor's disguise, had everything I needed. The luck was that he was in Djibouti, desperate to get another boat. I later learned it wasn't possible for him to step foot on land anywhere in the world as Interpol was after him. I was the only sailboat in the harbor.

He needed me, and I needed him.

Luck.

The other German, Klaus, a gentle and sweet forty-year-old, appeared in Rhodes Harbour at the moment I needed a sophisticated electronics engineer as much as I needed radar on a dark night on a strange coast.

A word about Greek (and Turkish and Russian and Israeli and Italian and, yes indeedy, American and even German) electronics "specialists." They all claim to be all-knowing. In my experience, every electronics guy was the opposite, all-unknowing, except that all knew how to run up big bills. Most would jury-rig your problem so that it appeared solved for a few hours. They then depended upon your sailing off and never returning to their port, thus escaping responsibility for their butchery.

Klaus was the only living exception I'd discovered in twenty years of circumnavigation. He'd learned his electronics in a nuclear power plant in Germany, and he'd quit and gone to sea because even the towering technical standards of a German nuclear installation weren't good enough for Klaus. He knew only how to do things right. *Alles in ordnung*—everything in order—was his mantra.

He was an angel with a box filled with ICs, resistors, and other mysterious minis that only manufacturers know anything about. In three days Klaus repaired my GPS, my SatNav, my loran, my obsolete wind-water instruments for which replacement parts were no longer available, and my inverter, which no one I had ever met at sea wanted to touch. He also repaired my faith in technicians.

When we sailed from Rhodes our control panel looked

like a Christmas tree. All of the little red and green LEDs were flashing away in paeans of joy for Klaus's knowledgeable ministrations.

Luck.

It was night, and the wind was blowing 25 knots from the wrong direction over the shallow and unfriendly Aegean. My main ripped out its second reef, and we were motor sailing, inadequately, with the third.

The seas were tuned to the length of my waterline, requiring engine power to at least hold station. It's a moment at sea when every system must work perfectly, or else one must turn tail and return, if it's possible, ignominiously to the port in which we had just waved a brave farewell to other boats. Anything is better than that.

The saltwater pump chose that moment to seize and rip up the spline on the pulley. The pulley flew off in one direction, and its precious, irreplaceable reverse-thread nut disappeared in another. The fan belt, of which I had no spare, fell victim to all this mayhem.

The temperature reached 212°F before we sensed the trouble and cut the engine. Not soon enough to prevent the plastic Vetus muffler, bought ten years prior, from melting down.

The list of what we needed to make en route repairs was disheartening. Where would we find a new water pump? Would we be able, in lurching seas, to recover its irreplaceable nut? Did we have a spare belt? And most unlikely of all was the muffler. Nobody carries a spare muffler.

So what has this all to do with luck? Let me detail the improbable events that concatenated, luckily, at that moment into repairs en route:

1. Five years previously we had installed a new saltwater pump in Egypt. In a land where engineering is the mummy's curse, we were about to heave-ho the old pump when an Egyptian workman with a Third World horror of throwing *anything* away offered to repair the old pump. We agreed, mostly not to seem arrogant of his kind offer, and we buried the "repaired" pump deep in other assorted and unused debris and promptly

forgot about its existence. When, in exigent conditions, five years later, we retrieved the despised item, it worked perfectly. Certainly not foresight. Pure luck.

2. The nut was found teetering precariously on the edge of our bottomless bilge. Luck.

3. The only fan belt aboard that fit the water pump was the one that ran our fridge compressor, with which we could easily do without. (In fact, we deep-sixed the fridge, a useless drain on our power supplies when we used it, which was practically never anyway.) Luck.

4. Ten years previously, when our stainless muffler gave up the ghost, as they all do sooner rather than later, I was urged to replace it with the then newly developed plastic Vetus. I was very uncomfortable and raised the question with Vetus as to what would happen in case it should melt down.

This query was met with gales of Swedish laughter. Impossible. Short of the bilgewater catching fire (ho-ho), the muffler would last forever.

I was still uncomfortable with a plastic muffler so they suggested that if I was so much of a Milquetoast mariner, perhaps (ha-ha) I should buy a spare. This suggestion, made in purest jest, sounded OK to me, and I left with two Vetus mufflers. The Swedes were convulsed.

Ten years passed; my Vetus muffler melted down, and *I had a spare muffler aboard*. Nothing could be more unlikely than a spare muffler.

I felt like Frank Lloyd Wright, who had demanded a moat for fire-fighting water around his Imperial Hotel in case of earthquake. Amid polite Japanese laughter he was allowed to have his way. Of course, the earthquake happened, the water supply failed, Tokyo burned to the ground, but Wright's Imperial Hotel survived.

A sailor with more hubris would ascribe to all of these events the label of careful planning. Cow chips! Luck, pure luck.

I have an Israeli friend, a pilot, who at age sixty-five had decided to earn a Guinness World Record by flying and floating in the sky in every device that could remain aloft. In the course of a few years he flew everything from an F-16 to a 747 to the smallest single-engine Cub and onward down from that to ultralights. Then he ballooned, kited, and glided. He needed only a parachute jump to complete his list. He epitomized my perfect vision for old age. To wit: put yourself in harm's way, and never let dusty decades interfere with your life.

He took his parachute aloft, and at 8,000 feet he launched his ancient Jewish bones into the blue sky and whooped his way down toward Jerusalem to about 3,000 feet, where he pulled his rip cord. His chute streamed out after him but failed to open. At increasing velocity he hurtled earthward, ruing the fact that now, with his demise, he would miss the record book.

At 50 feet from becoming an unseemly splotch on the Holy City, his chute caught on the cornice of a three-story building, where he bounced up and down like a yo-yo to a stop, breaking some unimportant bones and disturbing some muscles. While he didn't walk away from this landing, he was carried away chortling.

I call that luck of a very special caliber.

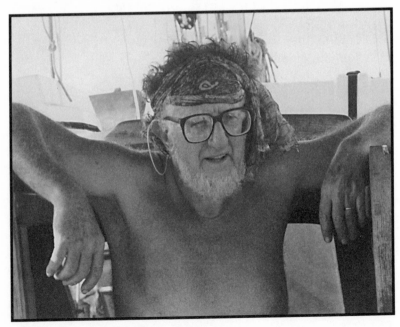

As I got older and more at risk, each time I set out on a passage my daughter Diane managed to gift me with amulets and charms of increasing powers from different cultures. Once it was a miniature lucky mask from Bali, once it was a set of seven Japanese gods carved on grains of rice, once it was the Hebrew letter for eighteen, *C'hai*, the sign for life, and once it was a pair of silver Apache "tall men" in honor of my half-Apache grandson. Is Diane superstitious? Heaven forbid! She's simply taking no chances with my luck.

When we were in Bombay, a sailor friend, Gulshan Rai, who made his own circumnavigation (a rarity among Indian sailors), gave me a sandalwood image of the elephant god of good luck, Lachshmi. Was modern, rational Gulshan superstitious? May the gods forbid! He simply wasn't taking any chances with my luck.

While in the course of decades of sailing about, I have off-loaded and replaced almost everything on my boat, but Lachshmi and the amulets, like the Vetus muffler, remain. Am I submitting to superstition? Do I believe in divine intercession? Lord knows, I don't. I'm simply not taking chances with my luck.

And neither should you.

Remain *bonus avibus*—under favorable signs.

Now Hear This

In spite of my great age, I love the Beatles and think Michael Nesmith is the cat's meow. I also know that there's nothing wrong with my hearing, because I recently went to my friendly audiologist who notified me in round and modulated tones (which professionals always seem to affect) that my hearing was somewhat better than I deserve for my age.

But my good hearing is being abused by a modern curse. Wherever you go, the taxi in which you leave your home, the elevator that takes you up to the fancy restaurant, and in the fancy restaurant itself, you are submerged in unwanted background music.

I can't figure out its purpose. No one listens, and the net effect is to cause your table to raise their voices to be heard over the music. Immediately when this happens the folk at the next table escalate their voices and so on around the room until everyone is shouting. You would think that the maître d', hearing his background music drowned out by the shouted conversations of his diners, would then lower the volume. But, no siree, what he does is turn the volume up another notch to drown out the conversational din, and suddenly it is auricular nuclear war.

Things get worse as you get older. Not only do timpani abuse more, but your patience with the young and their predilection for clamor has long since fled you. Often, to the dismay of my children and other young friends, I've turned on my heel and exited the brutalizing cacophony that met me as I entered an eating place. Remember that phrase, "eating place," not deafening place, not hollering place, but eating place. Restaurateurs, being a generation younger than I, have forgotten that the ideal condition for digestion, especially elderly and civilized digestion, is the soft tintinnabulation of wine glasses and the warm tinkle as a fork is laid to dish. All of these lovely eating sounds should float just below the hum of congenial conversation.

It was this horror of perseverative, insistent, unlistened-to music that urged me to the sea, where I could pull into a cove for the evening and listen to my own thoughts or, if my thoughts displeased, to the comforting splatter of the surf on the shore, which never displeases.

On my vessel I'm king of the airwaves. I can ban rap and drift back some years to the dulcet and agreeable tones of Ella, who started it all anyway with scat long before the rappers were born if, indeed, they came into this world via biology, or were they spewed out of some giant, clamorous tuba in full and incomprehensible throat?

Alas, nowanights, too often when you seek the comfort of quiet after a day of sailing in abusive sun and screaming winds, your neighbor is likely to have his stereo blasting even before his anchor goes in. It's possible to privately enjoy disco, rock, punk, and death music in your home on land. Since a boat is nothing more than a reverberative and highly efficient sound box, there's no such thing as listening privately.

Showing my age, I let the ballads of my youth unremind me of the decades that have passed. "Stardust" and "Flying Down to Rio" beat the pants off of some ignoramus advising us to go out and kill a cop. When I so choose, I allow Bach and Scarlatti to enchant me with their musical mathematics so effective in cooling the unregenerate passions of our time.

My vessel, and yours, are the last places on Earth that the God-given right to listen to what we damn well choose is inviolable. With all of the other pluses that a sea passage gives to old bones, perhaps the gentlest is the soothing of the tiny old bones of the ear.

Not a few of the miscreants who blast the quiet of a cove with their go-fast boom boxes are the very same ones who are "against pollution" and in favor of protecting endangered species. Allow me to inform them that, after considerable research, I've determined the pollutive effect of loud music at anchor is every bit as intrusive as a pound and a half of mercury. And if I, in my eighth decade, am not quintessentially an endangered species, then what is?

This Old Man and the Moon

One afternoon, a few days after the United States made the first manned landing on the moon, I found myself tacking a map of the Earth onto a wall in a room in my house. I remember being in a state of high exaltation from seeing the unforgettable images of the first moonwalk. I was full of a sense of participation in a historic moment. During my lifetime, during those few years that I walked this world, my species, my country, was walking on the moon. We had made that "great step for mankind."

The headiness of the time, the feeling of adventure and discovery that washed over me, churned up ancient desires that I'd thought were long buried. Suddenly, nearing the end of my promised four score, I yearned for adventure: the moon, the stars, and beyond.

Curiously, though, the map I felt compelled to pin up was not of the heavens. It was a large map of our Earth, courtesy of National Geographic. It was so high and wide that I had to bump a lot of stuff off the wall and out of the room (the chart room, as I later came to think of it) to make a place for a world now shrunk to include the infinite parsecs of space.

I was puzzled by my actions and bewildered by my motives. There it was on the chart, the blue and green of the seas and the dark brown tops shading of land bleaching down ever paler until they met the lightest aquamarine of the oceans. It was, in fact, mostly ocean. This Earth was not, like space, beyond my reach. Every tone, every line, every inch and mile and fathom were mine, available, accessible, and free.

As I stood there that day, just a decade after Jack Kennedy had made his promise that man would stand on the moon, I suddenly felt somehow diminished, somehow cheated. In space we would never be free of the machines that took us there, the machines that fed and aired us and hurtled us there and the machines that brought us back to our small Earth.

The triumphant walk did not grow out of man's relation

to himself; it grew out of his relation to the machine. This was not satisfying for me. Even the unforgettable footstep itself was not man's, but some ribbed and bloated imitation of the elegant and useful human feet that carried us, with little mechanical help, from home to antipode and from Greenwich back to Greenwich. In space we sought freedom from Earth and found only slavery to the machine.

I now knew why I had unfurled that map of the world. I now knew why I was yearning toward the blues, the deepest blues of the deepest oceans. I wanted to be free, and a voice deep in my racial and biological memory was reminding me that freedom, especially for old men like me, lay not in space and not in the crowded accents of foreign lands and certainly not in the comforting lisps of home. Real freedom lay only in the empty seas and in the confrontation and communion with self.

It was on that day, already way past my prime, in a dreamy moment and without conscious decision, that I started my first offshore passage. I began to turn my dream into a reality in short digestible bites, one at a time. Swallow one, bite off the next. It's easy.

I invite all of you ancients, sailors or not, with similar itchiness to probe the outlandish, unthinkable reality of finding yourself in a small boat whose bows are firmly set toward the open ocean.

It may seem unlikely, but it's not unreal. It was, in fact, possibly the only course that I could take to save my soul.

To Hell in a Handbasket

James Boswell, biographer to Samuel Johnson, was of the opinion that anyone who would willingly go down to the sea in ships would "go to Hell in a handbasket."

Handbaskets were, and still are, the traditional method of carrying kittens, puppies, and babies, all of whom are more or less mindless and all of whom are acquiescent to other people's agendas. Thus, being carried about in a handbasket is a will-less, and in Boswell's mind, stupid and naive, exercise.

In his day there were no pleasure boats, only boats fraught in peacetime with hardship (a nautical term itself) and in war with death and destruction. Maritime agonies associated with trade and war had clear purposes: conquest and money. Down through history our species has been willing to sacrifice limbs, health, and life itself in its grasp for land and riches. In this light, subjecting oneself to almost certain death, abuse, and disease at sea had within it a semblance of rationality.

Had there been pleasure boats in Boswell's century, into which sailors willingly placed themselves, he would most certainly have invented a more vituperative aphorism. It was inconceivable to him that, even for power and money, otherwise sane folk would make the insane choice of the sea. Absent these rewards, the last scintilla of explanation could only have been dementia.

In this century things have changed a bit. In our time, recently as we shall see, the odds for survival have been twisted in favor of the sailor. But the threat of a concatenation of evils that can easily overwhelm a sailor is an ever-present and fearful concern. The things that can happen in a small boat on a big ocean, the unforeseeable things that no amount of planning can ameliorate, still lurk in the seas of our own times awaiting a fatal lapse of spirit, resolve, or strength or the equally threatening failure of gear or hull.

What has improved is communication, primarily effective

for short-range rescue operations. It wasn't until as recently as twenty years ago that short-range, line-of-sight VHF came into common use. Until then we were still in the 1700s, when an inverted ensign or a white flag or a "ball over a square" was the only way to communicate ultimate distress. Those of you who've been to sea, in even moderate weather, know how invisible a small boat is and how unlikely a pennant or flag signal of any kind will be seen.

In short-range rescue operations we've come a very long way. Via VHF radio (see page 72) we've now evened the odds in our favor, up to about a 10-mile range. After having attracted the attention of a passing vessel by VHF, we can go about that terribly delicate business of getting people from a small cockleshell, leaping about in a turbulent sea, ten stories up onto the deck of a big ship that's itself leaping and plunging three stories at a time.

We've even been able to extend the range by EPIRB (see pages 57–58 and 73), in which automatic radio-signaling equipment, cheap and small, extends the range of our yelp for help from 10 to 100 miles. If we have time in an emergency, a very big "if," a small boat at sea has the likelihood of being located within tens of hours. If you're already in an almost invisible raft, tens of hours can seem to be, and indeed, can be, tens of days. Survival is now very much a function of the length of time that the sailor can survive after a calamity.

Calamity remains a measurable risk. Calamities, both recorded and unheralded, claim sailors' lives each year. But the human spirit is such that the threat of death in the pursuit of life has never had much effect on our activities. Everything that we do that has in it the essential kernel of excitement, without which we obviously can't live, has in the background the ignored possibility of death. Ultimately, we humans, caught in the irony of our nature, require the acknowledgment of death to remind us that we are alive.

Sailoring is no different than other irrational activities and a damn site safer than most. Motorcycles take vastly more lives each year than does the sea, and a morbid list can be extended through the looniness of racing fast vehicles all the way down to the death wish of those using injectable drugs.

No. It's not the threat to life that makes sailoring so implausible. That threat has already been discounted by the nature of the way we play. It's not the danger that carries those of us who sail "to hell in a handbasket." It's other stuff, totally foreign to our true natures and inexplicably embraced by sailors, mountain climbers, and those strange souls who choose to give their feet to frostbite and their eyes to snow blindness in the walks across the poles.

It's the acceptance of discomfort by sailors who still go down to the sea in small boats that puzzles people, including me. Big events, such as the inevitability of death, we write off with astounding savoir faire. But most of humanity mounts an incessant and interminable battle against the small events of discomfort. Herein lies the puzzlement of going to sea.

From the invention of fire to the installation of room air conditioners, the central motivating force for most of humanity has been, still is, and ever will be the search, not for pleasure, not for the absence of pain, not for power and money for themselves, but, first and forever, for comfort. In all our complexity, we are a simple species. We yearn to be comfortable. It's in our nature. The reach for comfort is deep in our genes and has been handed down to us through unimaginable ages by our aeonic relatives. (See also earlier discussion, Pain and Comfort, beginning on page 119.)

Consider your cat. Make her even marginally uncomfortable, and with a twitch of her tail she's gone. Consider the paramecium, alter the chemistry, even slightly, that this primitive being considers comfortable, and he/she/it is on its way. Do something distasteful to the receptors of a virus, and it will mutate, astoundingly change its entire self, to escape a new abuse. By the time pain appears to us, it's already too late for us to do anything about it, and we know it. Discomfort, therefore, the precursor of pain, is the savior of all life.

Sailing is the Antichrist of comfort. Sailing murders comfort. Sailing negates every carefully regulated system for comfort, built up over centuries and millennia. Sailing attacks even those physical gifts with which nature comforts us without our asking or our connivance.

Sailing is the pits. The ultimate discomfort of seasickness interdicts everything (see discussion on pages 58–59). You can't think straight, you can't eat, your bowels are distraught, and in some cases you can't even throw up. And forget about conjugating. Those slick ads that suggest that bedding your lady at sea is a new erotic high are written by large-gutted, pale-skinned copywriters who get dizzy in elevators.

Every sailor I have ever known is seasick, in one manner or another, for all of the time he's at sea. The trauma to our carefully regulated systems of balance and perception cannot be ignored by even the oldest salts. Most sailors have come to terms with this abuse of our inner ears, but none of us is immune. Inured perhaps, but not immune. The imperatives to levelness, balance, and, in the physical sense of the term, equanimity are unimaginably ancient. Location in space, up and down, and the drive for consistent verticality emerged some 500 millions years ago as we emerged from the sea itself. Our pre- and post-aqueous progenitors learned how to tame directionless existence, and we sailors, robbed of vitality and tortured in belly and bowel by seasickness, would require another billion years to learn to reaccept all the variations to verticality that exist in and on the sea.

Proof? Look to your goldfish. Heat up his water a bit, and he lists to port; if you add a pinch too much salt, over he goes to starboard; and his penultimate move, before giving up his fishy little soul, is to go belly up. Life, at least beyond the microscopic, is upstanding, vertical. In the face of this blindingly obvious fact, some of us insist on sailing along all atilt.

The contradiction screams for insight. What really is the payback for the scurrility of sailing? What is returned to us that's half so precious as the comforts we sacrifice?

The more romantic among us speak in cadent poesy of the mysterious gifts of the sea. The sea grants, they say, peace, perspective, and understanding of self. Some sailors, who've given themselves, their comfort, and their safety to the sea, claim that the sea enlarges and enriches their spirit.

I'm no romantic, nor am I comfortable with these anthropomorphist explanations. I don't sense the mechanism of transfer of delights from sea to sailors. The sea is the sea. Bodies of water that happened on this Earth much the same as mountains, grasshoppers, and ourselves happened.

I can look for meaning and intent only in the human spirit. Whatever happens to us as humans I can read only in the light of that ultimate mystery, our unfathomable minds.

In our minds, in our brains, if you will, lies the human spirit, and if our spirit sees some profit, as it does in sailing, then the inquiry must be directed inwardly to where pleasure and pain lie and not outwardly to the sea, which, in the scheme of things, doesn't give a damn.

In this context I can pass along only beliefs and feelings. I have no proofs, facts, or other befogging elements to explain why and how my years on the sea have paid me well. What I know about are the things that happened to me and their impacts on me. Perhaps the impacts are universal, a nice thought, but even if not, even if what satisfies me doesn't follow for others, it remains for me a tale of growth and expansion of my perception of self.

I have only anecdotes, stories.

But as a very wise man once asked me, "What is life without stories?"

So let's repair to that cozy and secret place in which life really happens, and talk a little fiction.

My Debt to *Unlikely*

She is called *Unlikely*, not an attractive name, because the first time I found myself on a serious sailboat on a serious ocean I was struck with the unlikely thought that I was on this cockleshell, at the mercy of forces that I didn't begin to comprehend, through a complicated series of absurd, implausible, and unlikely events that commenced as I exited youth and entered old age. Logic never intervenes in a life decision to go to sea.

Many sailboat owners, as distinguished from sailors, have boats primarily for reasons of image. They rarely untie from the dock, and most almost never go out at night. For these folk, sailboats, which have about them the smell of adventure, money, romance, and vitality, are a sexual pheromone.

Real sailors soon discover that our boats inveigle and beguile us to conform to *their* agenda rather than to our shallow, imagined concerns. Given the opportunity, our boats reveal to us a larger view with broader meanings than we have known and teach that, in the face of advancing age, a new life awaits us "beyond the blue horizons." Sailors become witlessly lost in the wonderment of our good fortune in being hoodwinked into a new and marvelous life. The decision to enter the sailorly life is a moment of epiphany, which just *happens*. Unlike most turns of fate, this happenstance is good for sailors and a life extension for old sailors.

Logic inveighs against entering the sailing life. Sailoring stands in proud distance from common sense. If we trust sweet reasonableness and "what everybody knows," we would never go to sea. Those without a strong thread of irrationality would never choose the sea. Chaos, confusion, illucidity, and general murkiness of thought are the prerequisites for serious sailoring. The only rational explanation, if you can call it that, came from a madman who climbs mountains. He said, "I climb them because they are there."

Your irrationality is matched by the irrationality of your

sailing vessel. Although perfectly attuned to the natural medium of the sea, all sailing boats violate their own logic. They are hollow in a medium that abhors emptiness. They are constructed of materials far heavier than the water they live in. They resist the sideways thrust of tide and current. Most obstinately, they sail against the wind.

The moment you come to understand that your sailing boat teeters on the brink of the abyss of natural law, that she violates every natural directive, in that moment you begin to understand the wonders of a modern sailing boat.

She's not so much paradigm as she's paradox, more contrived and bizarre in her mastery of the sea than most artifacts of mankind. She's a bundle of disparate contradictions.

Let me count the ways that I love her.

I love her for the manner in which she coddles and protects me. Since I've come to know her limits, which are vast, I feel no fear and can comfort those newly come aboard. One day I was sailing in the Virgins with my youngest daughter, Toby. As we came up on the high hills that protect Virgin Gorda, we were struck by a williwaw, a vicious little wind that falls off the face of high hills. My boat went over on her beam ends, and I looked down to see Toby lying in the gunwale. "Promise me," she pleaded, "that we will come up." I promised, and *Unlikely* did what she was designed to do and always has.

I love her for the separation she provides me from too many people, too much information, and too much interference with my head. When at sea she's my own private, circumscribed universe in which I can come to know myself. On my boat at sea, there's no one to sucker me with either praise or blame. My soul becomes as visible to me as are the glorious sunsets at sea. Soul and sunsets fuse into an otherworldly experience.

She allows me, in spite of the decades that press down on me, a prideful swagger when I go ashore. She separates me from most of humanity. She allows me to be exuberantly different. She requires that I do life, not merely view life.

From my vessel and from my sailorly life I distill, perhaps unfairly but who cares, a comforting, belly-warming sense of my own self-worth. Can it really be a sin of pride to discover, in our penultimate decades, that we sailors are better than most?

I think not.